NEW MEXICO

—— IN THE ——

MEXICAN-AMERICAN WAR

RAY JOHN DE ARAGÓN

Foreword by Former Governor Jerry Apodaca & First Lady Clara Apodaca

THE
History
PRESS

Published by The History Press
Charleston, SC
www.historypress.com

Copyright © 2019 by Ray John de Aragón
All rights reserved

Cover images: Author's collection and courtesy New Mexico Historical Society.

First published 2019

Manufactured in the United States

ISBN 9781467141314

Library of Congress Control Number: 2018966269

Notice: The information in this book is true and complete to the best of our knowledge. It is offered without guarantee on the part of the author or The History Press. The author and The History Press disclaim all liability in connection with the use of this book.

DEDICATION

This book is dedicated to historical and cultural phenomenon Padre Don Antonio José Martínez, New Mexico's iconic folk hero priest. In nineteenth-century New Mexico, Padre Martínez was known as "El Conciliador" (The Conciliator), one who serves to mediate between opposing factions or armies. This extremely dedicated Roman Catholic priest was constantly fighting for the rights of the poor, the oppressed and the handicapped. He was ahead of his time and place. Padre Martínez was a champion of the Native Americans, always looking out for their best interests. He firmly believed in the conservation of wildlife and the environment and fought for the disadvantaged. Americans called Martínez "The Grey Eminence of Taos," because he spoke out against the fur trade, the needless killing of animals and those who unmercifully capitalized on downtrodden people.

Padre Martínez began the first bilingual (Spanish and English) school in the United States around 1833. The marvelous priest added the arts, including music, dance and visual arts into his curriculum. He printed his own textbooks and the first newspaper in the West, called *El Crepúsculo* (*The Dawn*). This very popular cleric maintained an orphanage, and trained youth for the priesthood and young girls for religious orders. He promoted the learning of law and is credited with opening the first law school west of the Mississippi. Bishop Don José Antonio Laureano de Zubiria appointed Padre Martínez as vicar and ecclesiastical judge of Taos and northern New Mexico. The padre was an expert in civil law, and Americans, including

Padre Don Antonio José Martínez is considered New Mexico's folk hero priest who fought injustice in the church and society. *Courtesy Dora Martínez de Armijo.*

Bishop Lamy, consulted him in many cases. Several of the priest's students became successful attorneys and Mexican and American governmental leaders in Mexico City and Washington, D.C. The vociferous priest strongly stated his causes as a delegate in the Mexican National Congress. Native

Americans regarded Padre Martínez as a great holy man because he was a major proponent of their human rights and equality. The honorable priest helped to define the Hispanic New Mexican and national Hispanic American experience. He was thought of as a saint, yet he was maligned and, after his death, became a victim of calumny and denigration from outsiders and others who maliciously charged him as a womanizer and with fathering countless children. Hateful accusations were meant solely to destroy his honorable life and excellent reputation. His blackened memory still clouds the New Mexican horizon.

CONTENTS

FOREWORD

As we look back into New Mexico governmental and military history, we find there were several accomplished leaders. There was Congressman Antonio Manuel Fernández, as well as Senators Dennis Chávez and Joseph Montoya. In the New Mexico state capital, Miguel Antonio Otero, Ezequiel Cabeza de Baca and Octaviano Larrazolo were early governors. Each and every one served with distinction. During the Civil War, thousands of New Mexicans served the Union, and Lieutenant Colonel Manuel Antonio Chávez, who was a young cadet in the Mexican-American War, is recognized as a famous hero. Many soldiers in New Mexico's history were awarded medals, including the posthumous medal given to Daniel Fernández, who saved several of his comrades during the Vietnam War and received the Congressional Medal of Honor for his heroism.

Our New Mexico children and youth have much to be proud of and many to look up to. A good self-image and self-esteem can certainly be nurtured by much of our New Mexico history and our accomplished leaders. It is imperative that we know this history, especially when it comes to the Mexican-American War in New Mexico.

—Jerry Apodaca, twenty-fourth governor of New Mexico

When he was elected in 1974, Governor Apodaca became the first Hispanic governor of New Mexico since 1918. The New Mexico State Public Education Department building in Santa Fe is named the Jerry Apodaca Building. Former New Mexico congressman and governor Bill Richardson called Apodaca "a champion of education."

Hispanic women for the most part have been left out of New Mexico history books. This has been especially true when periods of war and military are written about. Ray John de Aragón brings to life the turbulent history of the Mexican-American War in New Mexico. When wars are recounted, it appears as though women did not take part in any events. Yet, in New Mexico, there were medicine women tending the wounded, providing meals for the troops and comforting the dying, all while placing their own lives in danger. These heroic women need their place in history, as they lost fathers, husbands and sons in battle. New Mexico Hispanic women have blazed trails in all walks of life—government, business, education, the arts and the military. There are many who most certainly serve as role models for our female youth. The myths this book shatters will hopefully lead to a better understanding and appreciation of the real history.

— Clara Apodaca, former first lady of New Mexico

Clara Apodaca served on the board of directors of the Museum of New Mexico. She also served as secretary of the New Mexico State Office of Cultural Affairs and on the board of directors of the Washington Performing Arts Society. She was also on the White House Millennium Commission. Apodaca was the president and CEO of the National Hispanic Cultural Center Foundation.

HISTORICAL SETTING

"Prayer On the Battlefield"

Smoke and dust are around me; the cannon are roaring,
And their death-blasts, like bolts from the heavens are pouring;
Their lightening is darting; the earth is all red;
I hear not, and see not, save dying and dead.
To Thee, oh Omnipotent! Humbly I bow, —
There is none that bears rule in the battle but Thou!

Thou only Omnipotent! Whether the sea
Calms her pride and her wrath, as she listens to thee;
Or whether thou biddest the dead from the grave,
Or speakest in battle, Thou only canst save.
Thou knowest, my Father, that dangers betide;
Be thou my Protector, my Saviour, and Guide.

Thou knowest, our Father, we war for the right;
To thee looks our country—oh, arm in Thy might!
Let Thy sword wave in front of our serried array;
Let Thy buckler be o'er us to guard, in the fray.
Oh Father, though I should in death be laid low,
Defend my loved land from the arm of the foe.

Yet spare me oh God! For the world Thou hast made,
Seems a garden of verdure in beauty arrayed:
Its charms around me—but if 'tis Thy will
That my grave be the battlefield, merciful still,
Oh! Take me where passion is banished forever,
Where from Thee, and thy love-smile, no war-shock can sever!

—*George Payn Quackenbos, June 13, 1847*

New Mexico played a pivotal role in the ultimate defeat of the Republic of Mexico during the Mexican-American War. Very little has been written about this military action of the United States that changed the course of history for the United States, along with the size of its territory. New Mexico was a vast area that stretched into most of the West. In fact, the extent of New Mexico was not precisely delineated in early Spanish, Mexican and United States maps that featured North America. However, it is known that it encompassed the areas of present-day Nevada, Utah, Arizona, New Mexico and parts of Colorado, Wyoming and California. This was the Spanish province of New Mexico, and later a frontier province of Mexico. Securing this territory and holding it militarily was paramount to winning the West and achieving President James Knox Polk's doctrine of Manifest Destiny. New Mexico held sway in commerce and trade for Mexico with numerous trade routes, including the Santa Fe Trail to Independence, Missouri; the Chihuahua Trail, the old El Camino Real de la Tierra Adentro (The Royal Highway of the Interior Land) from Santa Fe, the capital city of New Mexico, that veered all the way to Mexico City; and the Spanish Trail from Santa Fe to California. A large number of produced goods, livestock and metals, such as gold, silver and copper, were transported from New Mexico into Mexico and the United States. The Spanish Trail from Santa Fe into California, along with its military installations called presidios, helped to secure military interests and commerce in the New Mexico region. Very little is known about New Mexico's history during the Mexican-American War. But a history tainted by legend and myths has greatly impacted the ultimate place of the United States of America today.

In the May 2013 issue of *Smithsonian Magazine*, Tony Horwitz comments about the book *Bunker Hill: A City, a Siege, a Revolution*, by Nathaniel Philbrick, the controversial author of *Mayflower: A Story of Courage, Community, and War*; and *The Last Stand: Custer, Sitting Bull, and the Battle of the Little Bighorn*. In *Bunker Hill*, Philbrick essentially debunks some of the mainstream and

Left: A soldier traveling with Kearny's Army of the West drew a horrific battle scene somewhere in New Mexico, circa 1847. He signed with the initials *E.C. Author's collection.*

Right: Army of the West soldier E.C. drew a caricature of a girl supporting "The Mexican War." *Author's collection.*

iconic myths about the Revolutionary War and the beginnings of the United States of America. Horwitz writes that Nathaniel Philbrick came to the conclusion "in short, [that] the nation's memory of Bunker Hill is mostly bunk." For example, Philbrick writes that there are American monuments to American defeats and the place commemorating the famous Battle of Bunker Hill is at the wrong site. Philbrick states, "There's an ugly civil war side to revolutionary Boston that we don't often talk about…and a lot of thuggish, vigilante behavior groups like the Sons of Liberty." In his review, Horwitz finds that the freedoms the "Minutemen" have been romanticized as fighting for in the country's early history did not include the freedom of certain groups such as Native Americans, black slaves, Roman Catholics or women in general. Horwitz notes that near the site of the actual Battle of Bunker Hill is an area on maps for its more sinister reputation as an area frequented by prostitutes during the Revolution, marked as "Mount Whoredom." He also claims that a writer named Parson Weems fabricated much of what has been recorded in textbooks.

Other popular American myths—such as Paul Revere shouting "The British are coming!"—never occurred. Revere and two companions, Samuel Prescott and William Dawes, were arrested before the battle took place. The British patrol eventually let Revere leave without his horse, and instead of going to Concord, he walked back to Lexington. Henry W. Longfellow wrote the fictional poem about the ride, which was later used as fact in history books. Another popular story claimed Pocahontas fell madly in love with Captain John Smith, but that would have been outrageous. At the time, she was twelve years old, and he was twenty-eight! Camilla Townsend, a history professor at Rutgers University, states,

> *I think the reason it's been so popular—not among Native Americans, but among people of the dominant culture—is that it's very flattering to us… the idea is she admires the white man, admires Christianity, admires the culture, wants to have peace with these people, is willing to live with these people rather than her own people…makes people in white American culture feel good about our history. That we were not doing anything wrong to the Indians but really were helping them and the "good" ones appreciated it.*

And the real story is that American cavalry troops did not make a heroic last stand at the Battle of the Little Bighorn. Custer was soundly defeated in a triumphant victory for the Indians, yet Chief Sitting Bull was not honored with American memorials and monuments. Remember the Alamo? The historical record pretty much contradicts most everything that has been written about proclaimed heroes that lost a battle in which they positioned themselves in a fortified Spanish Catholic Church and caused its destruction. These Texans were not fighting for freedom and their rights, as has been written, but to keep slavery alive in Texas and the American South. The Mexican government had officially outlawed and eliminated slavery in the territories of the country in 1829. These territories included Texas, which was still part of the Republic of Mexico. This act fiercely aggravated southern American immigrants in Texas. The end result was that Texas, after it became a state of the Union, vociferously and wholeheartedly joined the Confederacy during the Civil War—against New Mexico and the United States, where slavery had been eliminated.

New Mexico's history has also fallen victim to myths and falsehoods, especially after the Mexican-American War. It is written the first united revolt against Europeans by Indians in the United States took place in New Mexico in 1680. It is asserted that Native Americans fed up with the cruelties perpetrated by the Spanish organized a great revolt led by an Indian named Popé. However, Indian tribes in New England had planned an earlier massive revolt, which took place on July 20, 1675. This united Indian revolt was led by Wampanoag chief Metacomet and included the Narragansett, Nipmuck, Pocumtue and Wampanoag against English colonists. Many English settlements were burned to the ground, and countless settlers were killed. The English, in a counterattack and in retaliation, killed hundreds of Indians in their villages and dismembered the body of Chief Cononchet, leader of the Narragansett. Metacomet was captured, killed and dismembered. *This was the first major revolt by Indians against Europeans in American history!*

Most prevalent in New Mexico history myths is that Kearny's Missourian force valiantly accomplished a bloodless conquest of New Mexico. It was not bloodless by any means. On October 5, 1846, Christopher "Kit" Carson made a similar false claim by saying, "California surrendered without a blow, and the American flag floats in every port." Several major engagements of military forces took place in New Mexico and California in which many soldiers from both sides were sadly severely injured or died from their wounds. It is said Western, or cowboy culture, originated in Texas, but it was in New Mexico where those *vaqueros*, or cowboys, developed cowboy culture and lingo, which was introduced to Americans arriving on the Santa Fe Trail. American immigrants were familiarized with rodeos, and they readily adopted and adapted New Mexican music, ballads and dances that became square dancing and other typical styles now called Western folk culture. Most prevalent in New Mexican myth is lore relating to the players, actors and events on the terrible stage of the Mexican-American War. During the Mexican War, New Mexico was filled with many bloody battles and hard-fought skirmishes. Whole towns were destroyed, and there were many unrecorded deaths of men, women and children.

Most of what has been previously written about New Mexico's history has to be rewritten, or at the very least revised. Much of the real history was purposely left out to suit those who were writing it, so prejudice, falsehoods and malicious statements meant solely to denigrate the people, the land and the leaders prevailed. Some of New Mexico's history was distorted by design. Some of the history was intentionally omitted and relegated to little-known footnotes. An editorial in the July 4, 1846 *Anglo American* (New York) presents the power of news during the Mexican-American War:

> *In the absence or abeyance of warlike intelligence, the mind is not suffered to sink into temporary repose, nor to brood over future tactics in the prosecution of the present war. The whirl and confusion of politics quickly succeed those of the battlefield and of hostile deeds…it is much to be deprecated that the press in every country should so far lose sight of its true dignity and usefulness, as to cater for deceased appetites, to minister to false tastes to mislead ignorant or unreflecting minds, with views of men and things false in themselves, and injurious in their tendency. But still more is to be regretted that this should be done—not from the false views of honest*

though mistaken writers, but—for sordid object of pleasing the many, and of increasing their own worldly gain. The weak and mistaken man, may yet be honest, and his ideas receive correction from stronger minds, who watch the progress of events; but the willful misleader so trains the course of thought that it is difficult to thread the mazes of duplicity, in which he seeks to involve those who confide in him, and still more difficult to prevent him from escaping by a retreat already provided by himself, like the hideous spider when his foul meshes are invaded by a power superior to his own.

As we have all done, we do now. We view this as an abstract question of state policy, and are curiously watching how it will operate if applied practically on this continent. We have recently seen that a sudden excitement can for a while be raised, but that good sense will in the end predominate, and that the vox populi, is not always the vox dei [Latin for the voice of the people is not always the voice of God].

In an article appearing in the Saturday, November 6, 1847 *Anglo American,* it is reported that Texas Rangers are advancing into New Mexico Territory and are engaged in battle in other areas of the Mexican Republic:

About a dozen of Captain Hayne's Texas Rangers, encountered some two hundred guerillas at Santa Fe, and dispersed them rapidly by the use of their Colt's revolvers....The feelings of the people are said to be strenuously opposed to any compromise with the American....The Texan Rangers, about whom apprehensions were entertained at last accounts, had returned safely.

Point Isabel, Texas, May 18, 1846...and the Telegraph is just 26 hours from Point Isabel. Captain Auld, of the Telegraph, who has had opportunities for obtaining correct information, has given us some interesting particulars in relation our army operations. Captain Auld thinks the whole number of our killed and wounded must amount to more than 300.

There are three Mexican prisoners having but one leg between them all. The condition of the brave and esteemed Captain Page is melancholy indeed. The whole of his lower jaw, with part of his tongue and palate, was shot away with grape shot; he, however survived, though entirely incapable of speech, only communicating his thoughts by writing on a slate, and receiving the necessary nutriment for the support of his life with much difficulty.

It is stated that he does not desire to live, but converses with cheerfulness and exultation upon the success of our army.

All our accounts represent the Mexicans as having fought on the 8th and 9th with the courage and desperation which would have reflected credit upon the troops of any nation.

PART I

MANIFESTED DESTINY

1

LAND OF MAÑANA—SHOCK AND AWE

The Mexican-American War was one of the most unjust ever waged
by a stronger against a weaker nation.
—President Ulysses S. Grant

Writers of history interpret, provide their take and say what they think protagonists and antagonists during historical events meant to say or do. The real words of those who lived through history speak for themselves. Actual words open up doors to understanding and explain what actually happened. Lieutenant J.W. Abert, in his report on his examination of New Mexico, 1846–47, writes about what he experienced while visiting and talking to the Natives:

> *We entered some of the houses, and the people received us with great gladness. They brought circular baskets, nearly flat, these were filled with a kind of corn bread, or guayave. It bears a striking resemblance to a hornet's nest; it is of the same color, and as thin as a wafer. The guayave they crumbled up between their fingers, and put into a second basket, from which we ate. Each family occupies those rooms that are situated vertically over each other; the lowest story is used as a storeroom, in which they put their corn, pumpkins, and melons, and other eatables. The fronts of their houses are covered with festoons of bright red peppers, and strings of pumpkins and musk melons, that have been cut into ropes, and twisted into bunches to dry for winter use.*

American Military Department of New Mexico. Engraving from *Santa Fe: Ancient and Modern*, edited by W.G. Ritch, Bureau of Immigration, Santa Fe, New Mexico, 1885. *Author's collection.*

> *These people appeared to be well provided with the necessaries and luxuries that New Mexico affords. They are quiet, and seem happy and generous. As we walked through the town, we saw them unloading their burros. Quantities of fine large clingstone peaches were spread out on the ground, as the owners were dividing the loads, so as to carry them up the ladders. And whenever we approached, they would cry out to us, "coma! coma!"—"eat! eat!" and point to the peaches. They generally wear the Navajo blanket, marked with broad stripes, alternately black and white. Their pantaloons are very wide and bag-like, but are confined at the knee by long woolen stockings, and some-times buckskin leggings and moccasins.…When we crossed the Rio del Norte, I met Lieutenant Noble, of the 2^(nd) dragoons; he confirmed the reports that Captain Burgwin and Captain Grier had gone down the river to assist the American traders, who were threatened with an attack by a body of Mexicans from El Paso. We also heard that Mr. James Magoffin had been captured, and taken prisoner to Chihuahua.*

A decade before Lieutenant Abert's report, the government of the United States was looking into taking over areas of Mexican Territory. One means to an end was to claim there might be a possibility that Indians who lived in foreign territory could one day cross into American lands and attack American citizens. It was advised there should be a preemptive attack on Indians residing in Mexican Territory. According to government documents pertaining to proceedings, the following was recorded in a U.S. Senate report dated February 19, 1837, by future president James Buchanan, then on the Committee on Foreign Relations:

A Santa Fe Couple, photo by H.T. Heister, carte de visite, Santa Fe, New Mexico, unknown date. New Mexicans relished taking pictures. *Author's collection.*

In affording this opportunity to the Mexican government, the committee would suggest the propriety of pursuing the form required by the thirty-fourth article of the treaty with Mexico, in all the cases to which it may be applicable…the president refused to recall the orders he had issued to the general commanding the forces of the United States in the vicinity of Texas, directing him to pass the frontier, should it be found a necessary measure of self defense; but prohibiting him from pursuing this course unless the Indians were actually engaged in hostilities against the citizens of the United States, or the undoubted evidence that such hostilities were intended and were actually preparing within Mexican territory.

A civil war was then raging in Texas. The Texan troops occupied positions between the forces of Mexico and the warlike and restless tribes of Indians along the frontiers of the United States. It was manifest that Mexico could not possibly restrain by force these tribes within her limits from hostile incursions upon the inhabitants of the United States, as she had engaged to do by the 33rd article of the treaty. No matter how strong may be her inclination, the ability was entirely wanting. Under such circumstances, what became the duty of the President of the United States? If he entertained reasonable apprehensions that these savages meditated an attack from the Mexican territory against the defenseless citizens along our frontier, was he obliged to order our troops to stand upon the line and wait for the Indians, who know no rule of warfare but indiscriminate carnage and plunder, should actually invade our territory? To state the proposition is to answer the question. Under such circumstances, our forces had a right, both by the law of nations and the great universal law of self defense, to take a position in advance of our frontier, in the country inhabited by these savages, for the purpose of preventing and restraining their incursions… it (is) the imperative duty of congress promptly to consider what further measures may be required by the honor of the nation and the rights of our injured fellow-citizens.

Several government leaders in the United States during this period were reasoning why the nation should expand its territory into areas that were controlled by Mexico. Some of the rationales included protecting American citizens, as was already evidenced from incursions by Indian tribes from the area called Indian Territory. Major proponents included Henry Clay, the famous American statesman who was instrumental in sponsoring the Missouri Compromise in 1820, which admitted and allowed Missouri to be a slave state. Southern states were eying New Mexico and the West

Santa Fe Trail American merchant.
Unknown photographer and date.
Merchants sold a variety of goods,
from "Snake Oil" to "Cure All's,"
with ingredients from snakeweed to
cow dung. *Author's collection.*

in anticipation of adding more slave territory to the country. Clay stated, "It was quite evident that it was in the order of Providence…that the whole of this continent, including Texas, was to be peopled in process of time. The question was by whose race shall it be peopled? In our hands it will be peopled by freemen… in the hands of others, it may become the habitation of despotism and of slaves, subject to the vile domination of the inquisition and of superstition." Thomas Hart Benton, United States senator from Missouri, added,

Extensive trade on the Santa Fe Trail can be said, had grown up to be a new and regular branch of interior commerce, profitable to those engaged in it, valuable to the country from the articles it carried out and for the silver, furs, and mules it brought back, and well suited to the care and protection of our government.

Although there were many governmental officials and politicians who favored the purchasing or annexation of territories, there were those who questioned the methods of appropriation. As a member of Congress, future president Abraham Lincoln questioned the motives and intentions of mounting an attack into Mexican territory. Once an actual attack took place, he wanted an accounting as to why this was necessary. In a speech delivered at the House of Representatives on January 12, 1848, Lincoln emphasized,

The war with Mexico was unnecessarily and unconstitutionally commenced by the President…the President sent an army into the midst of a settlement of Mexican people, who had never submitted, by consent or by force, to the authority of Texas or the United States…to involve the two countries in a war, and trusting to escape scrutiny, by fixing the public gaze upon the exceeding brightness of military glory—that attractive rainbow, that rises in showers of blood—that serpents eye, that charms to destroy he plunged into it, and has swept, on and on, till, disappointed in his calculation of the ease with which Mexico might be subdued, he now finds himself, he knows not where.... When the war began, it was my opinion that all those who, because of knowing too little, or because of knowing too much, could not conscientiously approve the conduct of the President, in the beginning of it, should, nevertheless, as good citizens and patriots, remain silent on that point, at least till the war should be ended.

In a follow-up statement, former president Andrew Jackson proclaimed, "If Mexico had insulted our national flag, invaded our territory or interrupted our citizens in their legitimate occupations that are guaranteed by treaty, then yes our government could feel insulted and immediately administer a deserved punishment. But it does not appear that Mexico has committed any of these offenses."

Journalist Horace Greeley (1811–1872), founder of the *New York Tribune*, reflected, "Our course was taken in full view of all possible consequences and in the undoubting expectation that it would subject us to all manner of obloquy [disgrace] and execration [insult] from that class of patriots whose motto is 'Our country right or wrong,' and who believe in butchering men and starving women and children in vindication of 'National Honor.'"

When Andrew Jackson ran for president of the United States in 1828, he pledged to remove all of the Indians from the soil of the nation. At the time, there were approximately one hundred and thirty thousand Indians living in the states of Florida, North Carolina, Tennessee and Georgia. Once gold was discovered on Indian lands, the wholesale removal of the Native Americans began. When Jackson was elected president, he worked tirelessly to enact a law for the removal of the tribes to the west of the Mississippi River. He finally succeeded with the passing by Congress of the Indian Removal Act, which he signed into law on May 28, 1830. The immediate result of the

Masthead of the *Anglo American* newspaper published in New York by E.L. Garvin & Co., A.D. Paterson, editor. The *Anglo American* provided updates on the Mexican-American War. *Author's collection.*

enactment of the new law was that all treaties with Indian nations were declared null and void. The U.S. military was empowered to gather up and force march the Indians thousands of miles to arid lands far away from the homelands they had controlled for hundreds, if not thousands, of years. They were given very little food and had to endure exposure to harsh weather. As a result, many of the Indian men, women and children died along the arduous journeys, known collectively as "The Trail of Tears." The Indians suffered and died from disease, maltreatment from the soldiers and starvation. At least ten separate Indian nations were displaced. Most of the few Indians who remained behind were indentured slaves who helped Afro-Americans pick cotton. Some Indian women were married to white men, who claimed ownership of Indian lands through marriage.

President Jackson was quoted as saying, "True philanthropy is to the extinction of one generation to make room for another." These natives "were annihilated, or have melted away to make room for the whites… philanthropy could not see this continent restored to the condition in which it was found by our forefathers."

In James K. Polk's presidential campaign of 1844, the unpopular candidate pledged to spread and vastly expand the territory of the United

Presidential candidates relied on ribbons, buttons and all else to get their messages across. This ribbon shows Polk and Dallas, presidential candidate and running mate. *Author's collection.*

States. Polk was joined in his presidential campaign by running mate George Mifflin Dallas, namesake of Dallas, Texas. Polk in his term wound up being the first president in American history to govern a United States territory that stretched from the Atlantic coast to the Pacific coast. President John Tyler, the previous president, had signed the admission of Texas as a state, in a debated move on his last day of office. This controversial act not only set off the hard-fought Mexican-American War, but it also precipitated the horrendous American Civil War, a war fought for and against the enslavement of blacks and, incontrovertibly, American Indians.

President Polk sent American troops into Texas simply because the Republic of Texas laid false claims about its borders. The republic attempted to take over the significant trade and commerce on the Santa Fe Trail of New Mexico into Independence, Missouri. The war ended by fixing the Texas border with New Mexico Territory. This provided the United States with the opportunity to lay claim to New Mexico, Colorado, Wyoming, Arizona, Nevada, Utah and California. At the end of the Mexican-American War, the United States paid Mexico $15 million as compensation for this land. Another $10 million was paid for an area of Indian Territory in southern New Mexico and Arizona called the Gadsden Purchase. Texas was given $10 million for relinquishing all claims to this territory, including New Mexico. In 1849, American gold-seekers invaded California and New Mexico. In four years, by 1852, the population in California had risen from 20,000 to over 230,000. Levi Strauss invented his Levi's jeans for miners. Fugitive slave laws made it legal for slave owners to trail and capture runaway slaves in California. It was a fight between the North and the South. But how did this very powerful and overpowering effect begin?

2

TESTING THE WATERS

LEWIS AND CLARK

Both the United States and France set their sights on the vast territory of New Mexico. As a *provincia interna*, an internal province of New Spain, New Mexico was vulnerable. Viceroy Juan Ruiz de Apodaca in the capital city of Mexico was alarmed that the northernmost frontier of the Spanish Empire in the New World was wide open to attack. Spanish intelligence had revealed that foreign powers were very seriously considering an invasion and takeover of the territory because its boundaries were ill defined. Militarily, New Mexico had insufficient and inadequately trained troops. The soldiers in place were poorly armed and could not fend off an attack. This had to be shored up. The protection and security of the population, which included the Pueblo Indians, was a major concern for the viceroy. The borders of New Mexico had to be secured with a strongly armed militia, led by competent Spanish officers with enough munitions and arms to ward off any enemy. Lieutenant Colonel Facundo Melgares, the newly appointed governor of New Mexico, assumed this responsibility as commander of New Mexico's armed forces. His father-in-law was Lieutenant Colonel Alberto Maynez, adjutant general to the commandant of internal provinces; therefore, Melgares was very well connected militarily.

Facundo Melgares was a seasoned soldier who had fought in several campaigns as a member of the king's royal army. He was also familiar with Santa Fe and New Mexico. When the United States acquired the

Louisiana Territory from France in 1803, President Thomas Jefferson entertained expansionist ideas. He commissioned Meriwether Lewis and William Clark to lead an exploratory party of men to determine the extent of New Mexico's area. It was not adequately delineated on available maps. Lewis and Clark departed from St. Louis, Missouri, on May 14, 1804. Spanish authorities secretly learned about the intentions of the expedition into what Americans felt was disputed territory. As a young lieutenant serving in the presidio of Santa Fe, Melgares was instructed to search out and drive back Americans or capture them and take them to Santa Fe to be interrogated. Lieutenant Melgares had five hundred troops at his disposal to engage the Americans. He was instructed to fortify the areas of El Vado, Taos and Ojo Caliente. A highly effective Spanish military leader, Melgares was ready to meet the challenges of any foreign invasion into the territories of the province of New Mexico.

PLANNED INVASIONS

General James B. Wilkenson, who was the commanding general of the United States Army, was secretly planning an invasion of New Mexico. Wilkenson was involved in a conspiracy along with Aaron Burr, who is perhaps best known for a famous duel in which he killed Alexander Hamilton. Burr served as the third vice president of the United States from 1801 to 1805. During the Revolutionary War, he was an officer in the Continental army fighting against the British. Burr took an active part in General Benedict Arnold's military expedition and planned invasion of Quebec, in present-day Canada, on December 31, 1775. Arnold's army suffered many casualties and was soundly defeated at the Battle of Quebec. Arnold later defected from the Continental army and was granted a commission as a brigadier general in the British army. He then led British forces against his former comrades in battle. Arnold's name became synonymous with treachery, and he is regarded in American history as the personification of disgraceful conduct.

Alexander Hamilton referred to Aaron Burr as "a dangerous man, and one who ought not be trusted with the reins of government." Burr entertained thoughts of a Federalist secession of New York. He also attempted to aide Mexico in an overthrow of Spanish control of the Southwest with the seat of power based in Santa Fe, New Mexico. Lieutenant Zebulon Montgomery

Pike was sent by General Wilkenson on July 15, 1806, with a military force to investigate Spanish towns in New Mexico. The men started on their march to New Mexico from a base in St. Louis, Missouri. Wilkenson was interested in finding out about Spanish military weaknesses in preparation for a possible invasion. Pike and his force were instructed to disguise themselves as merchants and traders if they should be caught. Upon entering into southern Colorado, Zebulon Pike and his force were captured. They had built a makeshift fortress and had raised the American flag in an attempt to lay claim to the area and seize the territory by expanding the limits of the nation's boundaries based upon the Louisiana Purchase from France. A detachment of Spanish presidio soldiers from Santa Fe had been tracking Lieutenant Pike and his group. Spanish officials interrogated Pike and his men in Santa Fe.

American lieutenant Zebulon Montgomery Pike was sent with a force to investigate Spanish New Mexico military. He and his troops were arrested for espionage. *Author's collection.*

Since Zebulon Pike and his force had entered New Mexico illegally, Lieutenant Facundo Melgares and his troops escorted them to the military command center located in Chihuahua, Mexico. The Americans were imprisoned there for several months. Pike and some of his men were eventually released back into United States territory. Sergeant William Meek was detained for murdering Private Theodore Miller while in prison. Lieutenant Pike would write about the experience of his military mission: "For those men have served with me a long year and notwithstanding they are such Dam'd Rascals that you could keep no Ducks or fowls for them, yet I think them very clever fellows." Pike was implicated as an accomplice in General Wilkenson and Aaron Burr's plot, but nothing came of it since there was no definite written proof of wrongdoing on his part. It was claimed Pike was merely following orders to locate the tributaries of the Arkansas and Rio Grande Rivers. His detailed notes were used in later years by a Missouri expeditionary force to invade New Mexico.

In 1807, Aaron Burr was arrested and charged with treason. President Jefferson sought to have Burr convicted, but James Madison, the secretary of state, exonerated him. Former vice president Aaron Burr moved to England, where he attempted to raise funds for an invasion of Mexico. Burr envisioned himself as the monarch of a new country to be established in the Southwest with the seat in Santa Fe. He tried to relocate to France, but Napoleon Bonaparte would not allow him into the country. French exiles living in New Orleans, Louisiana, were secretly planning their own invasion of New Mexico in 1817. Nothing came of this.

ENCROACHING THE TERRITORY

There were several military excursions commissioned by the U.S. government under the guise of scientific explorations. In actuality, these were attempts to redefine the borders of the young country. President James Monroe sent Major Stephen Harrison Long with a force to check into the Spanish borderlands around 1820. President John Quincy Adams succeeded in signing a treaty with Spain, but then the United States claimed that the Pacific Ocean was the new border of the country. There were disputes as to the extents of the Spanish provinces of New Mexico and Texas dating back to the Louisiana Purchase in 1804. The Spanish military had intercepted Lewis and Clark, who were sent to determine the best American route to the Pacific while trying to circumvent established Spanish settlements. Spain had let it be known that it did not want armed military infringements into its territories. Therefore, the Spanish military presence was significantly increased in New Mexico.

Hezekiah Niles, the most influential journalist and publisher of his day, reprinted a story run in the *Natchitoches (TX) Courier* before Texas independence, in his weekly news magazine, published in Baltimore, Maryland, on July 9, 1825:

> *New Mexico. From the Natchitoches Courier. A man belonging to an expedition fitted out for trading to Santa Fe, from St. Louis, in 1822, arrived here a few days since, by way of Chewawway [Chihuahua], Durango, and Saltillo, across the Rio Grande del Norte, by San Antonio, to Nacogdoches.*
>
> *He left Santa Fe in August last, and states that the trade of that country is lucrative, and the inhabitants friendly to the Americans. Wheat, he states, is raised in great abundance on the Rio del Norte, and transported on mules*

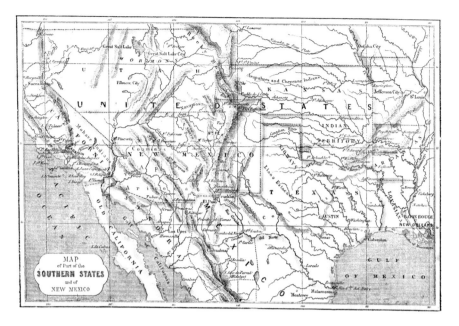

Map showing the extensive Territory of New Mexico and part of the southern states. Southerners claimed New Mexico as a future slave state. *Author's collection.*

to Guaymas, and other ports on the east side of the Gulf of California, from whence it is shipped, in exchange for silk, tea, and sugar, to China and India.

West of Santa Fe, nations of Indians have settled down into a state of civilization. They manufacture cloth, and various implements of husbandry and war. For the supply of their neighbors. They were not long since at war with the intendancy of Santa Fe, on account of the perfidy of the commander under whom they served in an expedition against the royalists, near Durango. Fifteen of their chiefs had been murdered, and they abandoned the republican cause for a time.

The new government has been completely established, and the condition of the country much improved.

Taos is the first town met on the route from St. Louis to Santa Fe, and contains 4 or 5,000 inhabitants. It is 80 miles from Taos to Santa Fe through a cultivated country. Santa Fe contains about 9,000 inhabitants, has some trade, but no manufactures. There is silver mine in its vicinity. One hundred miles further south, is Albuquerque, a town of some importance. The next place of note is the Pass del Norte, 500 miles north of Chewawway. Intermediately the country is inhabited and well cultivated.

Chewawway is a large city, containing about 30,000 inhabitants, and situated about 400 miles north of Durango.

To establish a military post at the mouth of Colombia River, the American government would find it much to their advantage to march their expedition by way of Santa Fe, to the Pacific, and thence along the coast to their destination. Five hundred men with 1,000 horses packed with flour and ammunition, can establish themselves in six months on the Pacific Ocean. The long and difficult way by the Missouri must certainly be abandoned.

One thousand horses can be purchased at Natchitoches for $20,000.

Meanwhile, Americans renouncing their American citizenship and swearing allegiance to the flag of the Republic of Texas included the famous Samuel "Sam" Houston. The first president of the Republic of Texas was embroiled in several disputes back home in the United States. He escaped into Texas territory.

New Mexico Alarm

Around this time, Padre Antonio José Martínez, the famed curate of Taos in New Mexico, wrote "An Exposition of Things in New Mexico" to President Antonio López de Santa Anna of Mexico on November 28, 1843:

At the time of the Spanish rule the foreigners from North America were not allowed to erect forts and establish commercial relations with the North American Indians, as the Spaniards were jealous that, under this pretext, they might cause some trouble with the Indians; but the liberality of our government allowed them to build such forts since the year 1832, near the shores of the Rio Napeste, del Rio Chato, and near other intermediate places between the plains inhabited by the Indians. But besides the useful and necessary articles, the traders sold the Indians also liquors and ardent spirits, which were prohibited. The result was that these Indian Nations became extremely demoralized, and were prompted to greater destruction of buffaloes, in order to satisfy their appetite for strong drinks, which they obtained in exchange. They also made raids in our Department of New

William and Charles Bent and partner Ceran St. Vrain established Bent's Fort and St. Vrain's Fort in Spanish territory as forerunners to an American invasion. *Author's collection.*

Mexico, in order to steal cattle which were bought of them by the proprietors of these forts, thus encouraging and inducing the idle and ill intentioned ones among us to follow their example, and become cattle robbers; selling their booty to the inhabitants or proprietors of the forts.

Ceran St. Vrain, of French lineage, who established one of the forts referred to by the priest of Taos, came from a family with a long history. His grandfather had deep associations with Ohio and the Spanish-controlled city of New Orleans. Jacques de St. Vrain was the commandant of the town of Nouvelle Bourbon in Louisiana. In 1799, the king of Spain appointed Ceran's uncle Charles as lieutenant governor of Louisiana. Ceran's father moved to Missouri. With the Louisiana Purchase, the United States acquired western territory that would later become the states of Missouri, Oklahoma, Iowa, Arkansas, Nebraska, Montana, Colorado, Wyoming, Kansas, Minnesota and Louisiana from France. All of this territory is what Charles St. Vrain served over as the lieutenant governor. The St. Vrain family switched allegiance from France to the United States and suffered various calamities that adversely affected their fortunes. This included fires, premature deaths and loss of resources. Ceran went to work for Bernard Pratte and Company.

Pratte was an associate of Charles St. Vrain and worked with Charles Bent's father, Silas Bent. This company was involved with trading furs and other merchandise for the Eastern markets. The fact that Ceran St. Vrain had a working knowledge of Spanish proved to be an advantage to reap financial rewards with trade in New Mexico Territory. St. Vrain was an early trader on the Santa Fe Trail harvesting rewards for the company.

TRADING AND TRAPPING

French fur trappers were traveling into New Mexico against Spanish policy, and into Indian territories, exploiting the United States' appetite for beaver coats, buffalo hides, fur hats and other commodities that were manufactured from pelts, leathers and furs. Profits for trappers and mountaineers were enormous. Ceran St. Vrain traveled back and forth from New Mexico to Missouri, attempting each time to build up a larger business. In February 1831, St. Vrain decided it would be to his advantage to become a Mexican citizen, while exploiting and capitalizing on his family connections to Spain, France and the United States. From 1834 to around 1839, St. Vrain succeeded in getting himself named as United States consul in Santa Fe. At this time, he formed a partnership with Charles Bent in a business called St. Vrain and Company. The next order of business was to establish trading posts, which were called forts, in or near Spanish and, later, Mexican territories. Backdoor intrigue, wheeling and dealing was the rule of the day. The partners first established Fort William, named after Charles's brother, in 1834, in an area of Mexican territory in Colorado. What St. Vrain and Bent established were fortified compounds that could eventually serve for American encroachment into contested territories of Mexico.

COMMERCIAL INCURSIONS AND BLOODSHED

St. Vrain and Company at Fort Bent spearheaded a vast trading business selling ammunition, weapons and other items to the Kiowa, Cheyenne, Arapaho and Comanche Indians. These tribes in turn committed depredations on Mexican settlements and among the Pueblo Indians of New Mexico, who were their mortal enemies. Spanish and later Mexican

Plan of the Route of the Expedition of Major Beall, 1st Drag's for the Relief of the Wagons of Mr F.X. Aubrey against the Apache Indians.
N.B. The Route is designated by dotted lines.

H.R. WIRTZ MED. STAFF. U.S.A

Ackerman Lith?, 379, Broadway, N.Y.

Map showing location of Bent's Fort and battle sites of Taos, Red River and Las Vegas, includes route of Major Beall of the first dragoons. *Author's collection.*

treaties with the tribes were thusly averted through a lucrative business that was conducted at Fort Bent and at Fort St. Vrain. Based on such a widely unanticipated success, the Bent brothers and St. Vrain decided to establish another trading fort in Colorado, and one known as Adobe Fort in a contested area called the Texas Panhandle. The partnership then hired a man named Richard Lacy Wooton, popularly called "Uncle Dick" Wooton, with heavily armed men to set up a toll road to charge travelers on the Santa Fe Trail to pass through from Colorado into the rest of New Mexico Territory through an area called the Raton Pass. This mountain pass, for all practical purposes, was the only accessible land area on the way to Santa Fe, so travelers, whether Mexican or American citizens, were forced to pay up or return to where they came from. Profits were enormous for St. Vrain, the Bent brothers and Dick Wooton.

On March 6, 1848, Richard Wooton married Mary Delores LeFevre, the daughter of French trapper Manuel LeFevre, in Taos. The marriage ceremony was officiated by none other than Padre Antonio José Martínez. Padre Martínez had also performed the wedding ceremony for the famous Christopher "Kit" Carson, who converted to Catholicism in order to be able to marry into a very powerful, wealthy and influential old Spanish family in Taos. Carson was virtually penniless, so he saw this as an immense opportunity to raise his position in life. This was a common practice among many other American men arriving in New Mexico who either abandoned wives and families back home in the East or left their longing American sweethearts behind.

In 1842, Major John Charles Frémont, of the United States Army, began a series of five incursions into the territory of the Republic of Mexico. The Mexican Republic had gained its independence from Spain in 1821. Kit Carson joined Major Frémont in his travels and led him as a guide. Carson gained his knowledge and experience of New Mexico territory as a resident of Taos when he joined Mexican hunting and trapping parties. While traveling in California, Frémont was involved in the Sacramento River Massacre. On April 5, 1846, he and his men used a howitzer to kill several hundred non-hostile Wintu Indian men, women and children on the banks of the Sacramento River. On May 12, 1846, Frémont and his men, along with Carson, were involved in the Klamath Lake Massacre, where other non-hostile Indian villagers were killed. According to Rebecca Sonit, Kit Carson was responsible for the murder of three unarmed Mexicans after Frémont told him the Mexicans were of no use to him.

Major John C. Frémont was eventually convicted and court-martialed for mutiny and insubordination. He had declared himself governor of California and called himself "Military Commander of United States Forces in California." His father-in-law, U.S. senator Thomas Hart Benton, appealed to President James K. Polk, who commuted Frémont's sentence and reinstated him into the army. During the Civil War, President Abraham

Left: María Josefa Jaramillo was the daughter of prominent and wealthy Taos merchant Francisco Estevan Jaramillo. She married Kit Carson. Padre Martínez officiated at the wedding. *Author's collection.*

Right: Army colonel Charles Frémont, an American spy sent to investigate Spanish territories for future conquest and United States expansion. *Author's collection.*

Lincoln appointed Frémont as Commander of the Western Armies. Due to insubordination, General Frémont was later relieved of his command by President Lincoln. Kit Carson became both famous and highly controversial for his mistreatment of the Navajo Indians in the so-called Long Walk.

In Mora, New Mexico, people were used to protecting themselves against an enemy. Republic of Texas troops claimed Texas was an independent, sovereign nation and that most of New Mexico Territory belonged to it. Texans attacked the peaceful village of Mora. Texas felt the United States government had previously claimed eastern New Mexico and now that area belonged to the new republic. Texan troops attacked in force to take over. Soldiers led by Colonel Charles A. Warfield took no mercy on the town or civilians. The bloody assault left many men, women and children dead, with dismembered bodies in the blood-filled fields. Young girls were kidnapped. Once the alarm went out, Santa Fe presidio soldiers quickly mounted their horses, and this ever-ready and brave cavalry pursued and tracked down the Texan force. A significant battle occurred. The Texans were defeated, and the women were rescued. Several related exterior events precipitated this very unusual attack on a peaceful village in New Mexico.

SECURING THE BORDERS

The Spanish government, and later Mexican government, were relentless in securing their borders from illegal U.S. and Texan immigrants that were trying to get into New Mexico territory. They strengthened the border patrols, and Santa Fe presidio soldiers were constantly on the alert. What compounded the problem was that American troops protecting American merchant caravans traveling on the Santa Fe Trail were always present. These soldiers were committed to protecting the safe journey of American merchants, and sometimes their wives and children who accompanied them as they journeyed to Santa Fe. The Spanish and later Mexican customs office located at the capital city was delegated with the authority to enforce the apprehension, detainment and incarceration of any American or Texan citizen attempting to gain illegal entry into the territory. This policy became more prevalent when Americans and Texans began circumventing the laws and infiltrated the borders under the auspices of the governments of the United States and the Republic of Texas.

In 1819, James Long, James Bowie, Jean Lafitte and Ben Milam set into motion a plan to invade and establish a new government in the Mexican territory of Texas. They met in secret in New Orleans, Louisiana, a former French territory newly annexed to the United States. Lafitte and his men supported and helped General Andrew Jackson defend New Orleans against British forces during the War of 1812. Bowie and Lafitte later joined forces as smugglers of African slaves for resale. In 1818, Lafitte and his men, who pirated Spanish ships, massacred the inhabitants of the Kawakawa Indian village on Galveston Island, killing most of the men and taking the women. Benjamin Rush "Ben" Milam was a lieutenant who served in the War of 1812. After recruiting an army, with the lure of potential wealth and free land all just for the taking, eager men including Milam joined James Long's force. They promised ten square miles of land to each recruit. The invading force rapidly grew to around three hundred men. Besides, with the Adams-Onis Treaty known as the Louisiana Purchase, the United States claimed the deal had included Texas and significant parts of New Mexico Territory as well. This was hotly contested by Mexico, but this gave Long and his men the excuse they needed.

Eli Harris, who led an additional army, joined the group in this venture. He went into Texas a couple of weeks before Long's army arrived. After securing an area, James Long declared himself president of the Long Republic, or Republic of Texas. He assigned a twenty-one-member

Supreme Council of his new country and attempted to set up trading posts. Jean Lafitte was promised the governorship of Galveston, but some believe he was a spy who provided information to Spanish authorities about the invasion. Spanish troops marched on Nacogdoches, and Long's men, who were low in morale and provisions, dispersed and fled. Approximately fifty men of the army were captured. The self-proclaimed president escaped, but he tried to raise funds for a second invasion. Long was financially supported by Colonel William H. Christy. Long led another ill-fated attempt to conquer Texas on September 19, 1821. His army captured the Spanish military presidio and town of La Bahia. However, he was later forced to surrender by Spanish troops. James Long was taken prisoner. Six months later, he was shot by a guard, presumably while attempting to escape.

A NEW REPUBLIC

Colonel William H. Christy had also served under Andrew "Old Hickory" Jackson at the Battle of New Orleans. He served as a staff officer under General William Henry Harrison and gained distinction fighting Chief Tecumseh and his Indian warriors at Fort Meigs, at the falls of the Maumee River in Ohio. Christy is regarded as the hero of Fort Meigs. He met Sam Houston, and they became lifelong friends after Christy was commissioned as a lieutenant in the U.S. Army. William Christy moved to New Orleans, where he became successful in various endeavors. After the Long fiasco, Christy supported Sam Houston in his takeover of Texas with money and funding the "New Orleans Greys'" recruits for the fight in Texas. He secured loans totaling $250,000 for William H. Wharton and Stephen H. Austin.

During his inaugural address to the Texas Congress, Houston said of Christy:

> *There sits a gentleman within my view whose personal and political services to Texas have been invaluable. He was the first in the United States to espouse our cause. His purse was ever open to our necessities. His hand was extended to our aid. His presence is among us, and his return to the embraces of his friends will inspire new efforts in behalf of our cause.*

The new effort for Colonel William H. Christy became to have Texas take over the Territory of New Mexico. On August 16, 1842, Texas

Republic secretary of war and marine George W. Hockley sent a letter to Charles Alexander Warfield advising him of a commission. President Sam Houston of Texas authorized expeditionary forces into New Mexico to expand its territory. Warfield's experiences in California, Colorado and New Mexico as a fur trapper were taken into account. He often worked out of Bent's Fort on the Arkansas River. He was also a son of a New Orleans merchant. Warfield was highly recommended as noted in the letter from *Senate Documents, Otherwise Publ. as Public Documents and Executive Orders of the United States Congress*:

> *Sir: Colonel William Christy, of New Orleans, has been requested to hand you the letter, with the accompanying commission as colonel in the service of the Republic of Texas…it is scarcely deemed necessary to enjoin that the strictest regard will be paid to the received rules of civilized warfare by all in the command….The will be considered in the service of Texas during the war, or until further orders; and the commander of it authorized to levy contributions, capture Mexican property or places, under the flag of Texas….The general route proposed will be from the rendezvous designated to Santa Fe, which with such towns as you may be able to conquer will be taken, and the property of the enemy secured. This, however, will not deter you from deviating from the route, should you find it necessary for the accomplishment of the latter object or for other purpose.*
>
> *One half of all spoils taken from the enemy will belong to the captors, and be retained for their use, and will be distributed among them by the commanding officer and his staff. The President will also make such appropriations of public lands, or those taken from the enemy, as may be placed within his control for that purpose.*

After gathering provisions, Colonel Charles Warfield immediately set out to recruit soldiers for his military campaign in Texas, Arkansas, St. Louis, Independence, and Westport Landing in Missouri. In Missouri, he succeeded in recruiting John McDaniel and his brother David. Warfield commissioned John as a captain in his new army. After gathering more recruits that included mountain men, and fur trappers, the group set out for New Mexico. Along the way, Warfield tried to convince other American citizens to join them.

The government of Texas planned a multi-pronged attack on Mexican territory to expand its borders. The Mier Expedition led by commander Alexander Somervell and his Texan army crossed into Mexico and captured the town of Guerrero. However, after a major battle with Mexican troops, and not receiving additional support and provisions for his troops, Somervell withdrew and disbanded his army on December 19, 1842.

Several of his officers were insubordinate and chose to continue with the initial plan. William S. Fisher took command in what is called the Mier Expedition, but his forces were defeated in battle. Many of his troops were captured, detained and later released after appeals from American and British government officials.

On January 28, 1843, Captain Jacob Snively outfitted a large force with the intent of attacking Mexican traders on the Santa Fe Trail while on his way to New Mexico. Similar to the conditions in a memorandum given to Warfield, there would be a division of spoils. The Texas War Department officially authorized the invasion on February 16, 1843. Calling themselves "the Battalion of Invincibles," Snively's men would rendezvous with Warfield's force and then proceed on their campaign. He and his men crossed and traveled into Indian Territory and United States territory that included areas of Kansas and present-day Oklahoma. Warfield and his men joined the Snively army. After crossing into New Mexico, they were met by Mexican troops and a battle took place. The battle was a draw, and Snively retreated. Warfield and Snively, plus their officers, argued about chain of command. The disgruntled Texan soldiers wanted to return back to Texas so Snively disbanded his army. Some of the men wanted to continue. One group of men calling themselves "Home Boys" selected Eli Chandler as their commander. Chandler served as the adjutant for Snively. He led his force back to the Arkansas River, where he and his men hoped to capture a Mexican wagon train traveling from Missouri to New Mexico. He and his men were seized by United State dragoons led by Captain Philip St. George Cooke. After being disarmed by American forces, the group returned to Austin, Texas.

DEATH ON THE SANTA FE TRAIL

It was on a peaceful day on April 10, 1843, that Don Antonio José Chávez met his fate. Antonio José was a descendant of one of the most distinguished families in New Mexico. His ancestors included the first Spanish colonizers in 1598, founders of several settlements, including the capital city of Santa Fe. He was related to family members who had served as governors of New Mexico. Another relative was future

A woman on the Santa Fe Trail. Sometimes, American women accompanied their husbands and were outraged seeing independent New Mexican women who spoke up. *Author's collection*.

lieutenant colonel Manuel Antonio Chávez, who distinguished himself as the hero of the Battle of Glorieta when his forces helped to defeat the Texas Confederates during the Civil War.

Don Antonio José Chávez was a highly recognized merchant and trader on the Santa Fe Trail who owned an extensive freighting business in Santa Fe. There were reports circulating around New Mexico that Republic of Texas forces planned to attack merchants from Santa Fe that were unescorted by the Mexican military into U.S. territory. Colonel Charles Warfield, after attacking the town of Mora in New Mexico and subsequent defeat by Mexican troops and capture by Cooke, apparently returned to his former life as a fur trapper. Captain John McDaniel and his men, who called themselves "the Mountaineers," gained notoriety for the capture of the Chávez caravan. Don Antonio Chávez and his party set up camp at the crossing of the Little Arkansas River on the Santa Fe Trail. They were on their way to Independence, Missouri, in several wagons stocked with a variety of merchandise and provisions for the long journey. Chávez also carried gold bullion and silver for his purchases. After a short fight with Chávez's men, Captain McDaniel's force captured the caravan and took everything as spoils of war. After some of the Missourian volunteers divided what they took, a few of them returned to their hometowns in Missouri. Captain McDaniel and his men took Don Antonio to a ravine, where he was brutally murdered. After this, they also returned to Missouri. The attack and murder created an international incident. Some of the group, along with McDaniel, were apprehended and tried for the crime in Missouri. The site of the murder was named Chavez Creek, and it was marked with a shaft of solid rock with the name Chávez carved into the rock. Sometime after the place was marked, the monument mysteriously disappeared.

President and General José Antonio López de Santa Anna is held responsible for the loss of over half of Mexico's territory. Unknown engraver and date. *Author's collection.*

On August 7, 1843, Mexican president Antonio López de Santa Anna issued a directive to General and Governor Manuel Armijo of New Mexico to close all of the customs offices to American merchants, which at the time were located in Santa Fe, San Miguel and Taos, and prohibit any further commerce with the United States. Missourians were incensed by this action on the part of the government of Mexico. Animosity in Missouri against Santa Anna and Governor Armijo steadily grew and was spurred on by newspapers such as the *St. Louis Reveille*. The economy of the state was dependent on this trade, as was a large part of the economy of the United States. The value of trade on the trail from Santa Fe and New Mexico to Missouri would have been in the millions of dollars annually by today's standards. President Santa Anna reestablished commerce and trade after U.S. government officials assured the government of Mexico that the Texan war party had been apprehended and that the Texas soldiers would be summarily punished, but the punishment never took place.

Colonel William Christy, due to his involvement in the Texan military campaigns, was charged in November 1835 by the U.S. government as setting up a military operation against Mexico in New Orleans, which was American territory. He appeared in the court of Judge William Rawle, but Christy used many of his political connections to his advantage to evade prosecution.

3

REPUBLIC OF TEXAS ATTACKS AND FAILS

The government of the United States to aggrandize itself by taking our rich department of Texas, and then advancing into the very heart of our country…
Mexico becomes the prey of Anglo-American ambition.
—President Antonio López de Santa Anna of Mexico

The groundwork for a premeditated attack on New Mexico had been laid decades before it actually happened. The Territory of New Mexico was seen as a prize that would help to expand the length and breadth of the United States from the Atlantic to the Pacific. During this period, it was all a question of adding slave states to the Union. There were those who were for slavery and those who were against. The revolt for independence in Texas against Mexico was a question of black slavery. The issue went back and forth as to when and who was to be controlled, as was attested to with the words of major and minor participants. For example, Sam Houston, president of the Republic of Texas, stated: "The Anglo-Saxon race must pervade the whole southern extremity of this vast continent. The Mexicans are no better than the Indians and I see no reason why we should not take their land."

New Mexicans were extremely concerned Americans and Texans settling in the territory entertained ulterior motives. Letters flowed into the office of Governor Manuel Armijo, including the following urgent communication from Rafael Antonio Luna dated February 10, 1841, and sent from Taos:

New Mexico governor and General Don
Manuel Armijo was a military hero who
was maligned and disdained by American
writers. Oil painting by Maximiliano
"Max" Salazar, 1980. *Author's collection.*

*C. Rafael de Luna neighbor of Taos, in required form and in the best way as
a right, under useful protests and necessary, and in the most immediate recourse
and our department so remote in the secular area, before Your Excellency I
present myself and say: in consequence of the death and estate of José de
Jesús Branch on the 27th of December of 1840, his widow, who is my
daughter, María Paula de Luna, so as not to express the responsibility of
the possessions of her deceased husband in the part that he had in company,
although that was a part of their own joint possessions and inheritances of
said daughter, I entrusted the keys, papers, and interests to two good men who
were Don Charles Bent and Don Julian Workman, naturalized citizens, so
that they as men of good fame and expertise in commerce and the management
of interests, would do what is convenient in this particular place, as judge
and whatever comes up in rights: It happened that Louis Lee who is one
that had an association or company with my deceased political son wanted
those interests placed at his disposition and Bent answered that it could not
be that way until it could be a legally transferred and said Lee filled with
uncontrolled violence sent to Santa Fe through Don Juan Bautista Vigil his
representative: he went and presented in Lee's name a request that an inventory
should be formed, and since then he referred to the first Justice of the Peace,
Don Buenaventura Valdez so that only he, at his orders would say how much
should be appropriated by this poor judge who had no practice in these matters,
much less as a judge, he has not ever done so in the community, in his simple-*

Letter from Captain Rafael Antonio Luna to Governor and General Manuel Armijo dated December 27, 1841, informing him of serious problems with Americans in Taos. *Author's collection.*

ness he quickly left the management to Vigil, he pretty much said that he did as Vigil told him because it was the law that he showed him in the book, and in this they were secure in their arrangement. In this circumstance, Vigil approved by Lee in cahoots with the judge, his director, to dictate the actions, and with the same judge, Your Excellency can see the consequence of what

47

was the result…he wants all costs to be incurred by the widow, and in this way she will be dispossessed of her property.…Today said judges, Baloes and Vigil are taking over the rest, and are evicting my daughter and her four children from her home.

A newspaper report appearing in the *New York Tribune*, published by Horace Greeley, on Monday morning, February 14, released the following:

Official documents have been received at New Orleans, concerning the capture of the Santa Fe Expedition and the subsequent treatment of the prisoners. It is clearly proved that they were induced to surrender by representations of one of their own party, Captain Lewis, that the Mexican force was much greater than it really was. They were also destitute of provisions, the country was impassable, and the Indians were hovering thickly about their camp. In this condition they were summoned to surrender, the Mexican leader assuring them that their arms and private property should be respected, and that they should remain in safety where they were, on parole, until provision could be made to send them back to Texas. Having express orders from the Texan authorities to avoid hostilities with the natives, they surrendered, and were instantly started off for Mexico. It was after considerable deliberation that their lives were spared. Ninety of the prisoners are known to have arrived in Mexico, where they are employed as scavengers of the streets. Mr. Ellis our minister there, had demanded the surrender of young Coombs, whose health is very poor, as a citizen of the United States. More than a week had elapsed, and no answer had been returned. Kendall had not reached Mexico.

The Republic of Texas invaded New Mexico. Traveling with the Texan army, American journalist George Wilkins Kendall recorded his experiences and forwarded these recollections to the press in the East. He later published a book bearing the title *Kendall's Santa Fe Expedition*, published in New York by Harper and Brothers in 1844, wherein he contradicts what he transcribes in the following communication to Greeley. In his book, Kendall states he and members of the Texan army were abused, mistreated, starved and forced to endure horrendous hardships. He also says some of the Texan soldiers were tortured by Mexican officers and soldiers. However, in his letter to his friends, including Horace Greeley, Kendall emphasizes how well-treated they were and how well-fed. He makes it a point to say that if he had a choice he would live in Mexico.

San Miguel del Vado, engraving by C. B. Graham, 1848. San Miguel held a Mexican customs house and military post. Texas troops were held here after their defeat. *Author's collection.*

The following letter, dated Chihuahua, Mexico, November 27, 1841, was received from Kendall:

> *My dear friends: You have doubtless ere this, heard that your humble servant was in what may be justly termed "a bad muss," but this the first time I have had a chance of letting you know myself.*
>
> *On the 15ᵗʰ of September last, after suffering hardships almost incredible on the prairies, in the way of starvation, &c. myself, with four others, were taken prisoners by a detachment of Mexicans near San Miguel, New Mexico. After a confinement of some five weeks at San Miguel, a town fifty miles from Santa Fe, I was taken and brought to this city with near two hundred of the troops (prisoners) attached to the Texan Santa Fe Expedition. To-morrow or next day we are all to start for the city of Mexico, where we shall probably arrive early in February, and where I have the strongest hopes of gaining my liberty once more, and soon after my arrival. It appears a little singular, does it not, that I, an individual perfectly innocent, and with no wrong intentions toward this Government, should thus be made a prisoner of and marched a distance of 1,800 or 2,000 miles? But at present we are all well treated, and I no reason to complain, although my case is a peculiarly hard one. One thing, however,*

I have gained by the operation—health, and that one of the best kind. I verily believe were I to enter the office in my present condition, you would not know me. I am stouter and heavier than ever I was in my life.

I have not seen a paper nor heard a word from the United States since I left in May last, with the exception of a rumor that war had been declared against England, and that the old Harrison cabinet had "busted up." Although I have been in the world for the last six month, I have not been of it.

My ankle, has nearly recovered, and perhaps you will think it time. So serious was the injury that for two months I was unable to put my foot to the ground. A broken leg would have been a mere scratch in comparison. There are a number of English and Americans here, who have treated us with great kindness. The Governor of the State of Chihuhua is also a gentlemanly and good-hearted man, and has done much to alleviate the condition of the prisoners. This is a place I should like extremely well if I had my liberty, as the people are kind-hearted and very obliging to strangers. At Passo, a town some three hundred miles from this, I received favors from the priest of the place such as would not be granted or conferred by any minister of the gospel out of Mexico—but of all this I shall speak further when I get home. Once more I say to all, keep "stiff upper lips." Tell all my friends that I shall "manifest" myself among them one of these days.

Hoping that you are all enjoying as good health as myself, I remain still,

Geo. Wilkins Kendall

In 1841, the Republic of Texas attempted an invasion of New Mexico. This poorly organized and poorly planned conquest was met with humiliating disaster. It is written the Texans never fired a shot and meekly gave in. They simply surrendered to a superior force that took advantage of them and maltreated them. Kendall wrote in his book that the miserable enemy forces from the Territory of New Mexico did not follow military decorum and abused the invading Texan army that only desired to establish a commercial trade with Santa Fe.

The facts: The Texan Republic was on the verge of bankruptcy and failure as a country. The republic was headed toward total collapse. In a desperate attempt to save the new nation, plans were made to take over New Mexico and its lucrative trade on the Santa Fe Trail with the United States. The Battle of Villanueva took place, in which New Mexican forces under

Governor and General Manuel Armijo and his officers built fortifications on the hills surrounding the only path to Santa Fe. Needless to say, the undisciplined Texan soldiers fell to the superior Mexican troops, who were well trained militarily. Shots were fired, and after a minor battle, the Texans surrendered. Several New Mexican military officers received medals of honor from the president of Mexico and commendations from Governor Armijo for the overwhelming defeat. A play, *The Texans*, was written to commemorate the victory. General Manuel Armijo was a hero, and he was assured a very positive record in history.

4
SUBVERSIVE WARFARE

Tuesday 25th noon. Mora creek and settlement—here is a little hovel, a fit match for some genteel pig stys in the states. It is made of mud, and surrounded by a kind of fence of sticks.…It's neighbors are smaller, far more inferior, and to them I have no comparison.
—Susan Magoffin, the teenaged wife of Samuel Magoffin, in her diary on one of her observations about New Mexico during her trip from Missouri to Santa Fe

Although the territory of New Mexico and the people residing there were considered "inferior," Americans saw it as a land of opportunity. James Magoffin, along with his brother Samuel, had relocated to Mexico. They had become naturalized Mexican citizens. This was not unlike many American merchants who moved to different parts of New Mexico to set up businesses. In fact, a few had denounced their American citizenships and had sworn allegiance to the Republic of Mexico. As Mexican citizens they were subject to the laws of Mexico, and were held to the same principles.

James Wiley Magoffin was born in Harrodsburg, Kentucky, in 1799. He served as the American consul in Saltillo, Coahuila, Mexico, from 1825 to 1831. He became a merchant, along with his brother Samuel. They dealt in cotton from Texas, furniture and clothing, plus other Texas goods. Around 1841, James Magoffin spearheaded a caravan of forty wagons loaded with merchandise, traveling from St. Louis, Missouri, to Santa Fe, New Mexico, along the Santa Fe Trail. It was about at the same time that the Republic of Texas sent a military force to invade New Mexico and take over its lucrative trading economy.

Henry Connelly
GOVERNOR AND COMMANDER IN CHIEF
OF THE
TERRITORY OF NEW MEXICO.

TO *Diego Archuleta*   GREETING: —

During the Civil War, Diego Archúleta, who aided the American takeover of New Mexico and promised a governorship, was commissioned as a brigadier general. *Author's collection.*

Magoffin's sentiments were ingrained in Texas, and he gave food, alcohol, smoking tobacco and coffee to the hapless Texan troops before they were marched to the Mexican military command center as prisoners of war—and eventually released back to Texas.

Mexican officials suspected that James Magoffin was providing arms to the Comanche Indians who were attacking New Mexican settlements. By 1844, the Mexican government placed restrictions on trade with Texas and the United States because of this. Magoffin's clandestine activities were at the crux of decisions made by the government. Generalissimo Manuel Armijo, commanding general of New Mexico's military forces and governor of the territory, enforced the restrictions placed on international trade. American merchants tried to circumvent these Mexican government policies.

AN AMERICAN SPY

James W. Magoffin was enlisted by President James Polk to start a subversive campaign to overthrow the Mexican government at Santa Fe. Magoffin became a spy for the United States. On September 27, 1846, he and four other Americans were arrested as spies in Doña Ana, New Mexico. Magoffin was tried and held in prisons located in Chihuahua, and Durango, Mexico, for close to a year. He was released through the leniency given by Governor Manuel Armijo, who intervened on his behalf.

The Magoffin Papers, a collection of papers, include a letter from U.S. secret agent James W. Magoffin to the Honorable Mr. [George W.] Crawford, Secretary of War, dated April 4, 1849:

> *To secret and personal services in the Mexican War under special engagement with President Polk, commencing from the 18ᵗʰ June 1846 when I left Washington City in the employment of the government until February 1849, being two years and eight months of time and extending to Santa Fe, Chihuahua, and Durango....The service being secret...of money received...was expended in bribes...as a Colonel of Cavalry, my duties keeping with officers of all ranks up to the governors and generals....I was engaged in June 1846 by the President and Secretary of War in the presence and with the knowledge of Senator Benton. The service and the engagement was acknowledged by President Polk, after I got back, in presence of Senator Atchinson and the only reason for not paying me was the want of money, see Mr. Atchinson's certificate, then Mr. Atchinson sent a resolution to the Military Committee of the Senate to inquire into making an appropriation for me. My papers were before the committee and no other claim, I am informed, and the $50,000 was reported to cover my case. Senator Atchinson has gone away, Senator Benton is going and I begin to feel uneasy about my compensation and beg your attention to my case.*

On April 1, 1849, Crawford wrote to former President Polk about Magoffin: "An appropriation was made at the last session for such services growing out of this claim."

Americans who had renounced their U.S. citizenship and had become naturalized citizens of Mexico were involved in an attempted overthrow of the Mexican government. This took place both in Texas and New Mexico. The Mexican government considered these men anarchists. Similar to in the United States and other countries, it was a crime to promote anarchy against the government and to interfere with the operations of the military. It was naturally illegal to support the success of the enemy, and any disloyalty to the Republic of Mexico was severely dealt with and perpetrators punished. No Mexican or naturalized citizen of Mexico was allowed to express opinions that were contrary to the good of the country and its people, nor could

Merchants, traders, bankers and lawyers flocked to New Mexico on the Santa Fe Trail, in search of land, profits and riches. Unknown photographer and date. *Author's collection.*

Magoffin fought against Major Jefferson Van Horne's decision to establish a permanent U.S. military post at the site of a Spanish, and later Mexican, presidio in Texas. This forced the removal of American military troops to Fort Fillmore, New Mexico. Fort Bliss in Texas was later established at Magoffinsville in buildings owned exclusively by James Magoffin, which he rented at a premium to the government of the United States—in addition to selling all of the supplies, merchandise and animal fodder required by the government. He also became the post sutler, a government position wherein he alone could say what could or could not be purchased for the fort.

APPROPRIATION OF LAND AND WATER

By 1852, James Wiley Magoffin had dealt his way into ownership of mineral and metal deposits in various areas of New Mexico. He basically controlled interests in common lands, which had been used by Hispanic residents and their families for generations, and water sources that belonged to all of the residents. He did not fail in convincing American sheriffs to organize posses to hunt down and prosecute anyone who infringed on his stolen lands and water rights. One twenty-eight-man group, led by infamous (or as some say, famous) Texan William Alexander Anderson "Bigfoot" Wallace, battled against over one hundred New Mexicans near a place called Chinos Road in 1854. Magoffin's Texans slaughtered the New Mexicans by using a howitzer provided to Magoffin's men by the U.S. military commander of Fort Bliss. Magoffin and his Texas rebels were indicted at Mesilla, New Mexico, for the killing of civilians. It was decided by the courts that the incident occurred beyond the jurisdiction of New Mexico; therefore all charges were dropped against Magoffin and his hired guns.

William A.A. "Bigfoot" Wallace had a wide reputation as a slave hunter. He would trail and hunt both male and female slaves who escaped their owners on plantations in areas such as Texas and the New Orleans region. Wallace was originally from Lexington, Virginia. He roamed through the South and finally settled in Austin, Texas, claiming to be an exponent of Texas's independence from Mexico. Wallace participated in what was called the Somerville Raid across the Rio Grande River, meant to attack and plunder Mexican villages. He, along with several others, was captured by Mexican authorities and sentenced to Perote Prison near Mexico City. This was a prison that housed hardened criminals. Southern congressmen fought for Wallace's release from prison, and he was finally granted amnesty by the Mexican government. One of his brothers was killed while fighting Mexican forces in Texas. After this, "Bigfoot" Wallace swore to "take pay of the Mexicans," which meant he would seek revenge. This earned him a reputation as a merciless tracker and killer who trailed Indians, blacks and Mexicans. As a Confederate soldier during the Civil War, Wallace was notorious for tormenting Union soldiers, tracking them down and harassing them. It is not known how many Bigfoot Wallace killed.

THE CONFEDERATE CAUSE

During the Civil War, James Magoffin became a staunch supporter of the Confederate States of America. In March 1861, as a Confederate commissioner, he forced the surrender of all U.S. properties in and around Fort Bliss in allegiance to the Confederacy. As a commissioner, Magoffin sold arms to the Indians and sought to get them to attack Union facilities. When the Confederate forces invaded New Mexico, Magoffin provided armaments, munitions, supplies, food and livestock to Confederate general Henry H. Sibley and John R. Baylor. New Mexican Union forces seized his properties in El Paso, Texas, after Lieutenant Colonel Manuel Antonio Chávez and his troops defeated the Confederate forces at the famous Battle of Glorieta. In the fall of 1865, Magoffin traveled to Washington, D.C., to request amnesty—citing his service to the United States as a spy during the Mexican-American War—from President Andrew Johnson. He did not succeed. However, Texas governor Andrew J. Hamilton appointed Magoffin to El Paso, Texas, on November 13, 1865, to organize a Texas militia and enforce a county government in that area. U.S. military authorities interceded. In 1866, Magoffin was granted amnesty and was restored to American citizenship in commemoration of his activities and service in New Mexico during the Mexican-American War as a noteworthy and highly distinguished American spy. Magoffin's previous denunciation of the United States, his support of slavery and his vociferous and financial support for the Confederate States of America were disregarded. In 1867, the Rio Grande River flooded its banks and swept Magoffinsville away. James Wiley Magoffin died on September 27, 1868.

5

A MISSOURIAN EXPEDITION

LAY OF THE LAND

Missouri was admitted into the Union as the twenty-fourth state in 1821. The area was originally a part of the Spanish Empire, with settlements and local governments. Spain opened up the territory to immigration to fend off British interests in taking over the area. In time, the territory was overflowing with primarily German and other European as well as American settlers, including famous Daniel Boone, known as an "Indian fighter." In 1800, Spain negotiated the Treaty of San Ildefonso with France, and it became French territory. In 1803, France sold Missouri Territory as a part of the Louisiana Purchase to the United States. The Missouri Compromise in 1820 allowed black slavery in Missouri. Within a short time, 40 percent of the population was made up of enslaved blacks. Indians were forced out of Missouri into Spanish territories to the west.

Ideas of expanding the borders of the United States, for all practical purposes, began with the birth of the country. Indian lands in the continental United States were rapidly being taken over. With the establishment of the Santa Fe Trail and growing commercial trade with New Mexico, plans were begun for the conquest of the territory. Parties of exploration to survey military forces were periodically sent out from Missouri into Spanish territories by the United States. Mexico's defeat of unsuccessful Texan armies complicated plans. It was finally determined to launch a three-pronged attack on New

This painting by C.K. Chapman shows the dress of Missouri troops and the uniforms of the Mexican/New Mexican military. *Courtesy New Mexico Historical Society.*

Mexico from Missouri. Missourian Mormon families would comprise one group to serve as a vanguard. They would travel in civilian clothes and in regular wagons. Two other separate forces, with one following the other at determined intervals and one leading the initial attack, would further help to confuse the enemy. It was not long before New Mexico officials learned about a possible impending attack.

Governor and General Armijo began preparations by issuing orders and military circulars. On July 11, 1846, he wrote to Colonel Pascual Martínez to contact the following officials: Padre Don Antonio José Martínez, the

Colonel Pascual Bailón Martínez led New Mexican troops along with other officers in response to the American invasion. *Courtesy Dora Martínez de Armijo (his granddaughter).*

colonel's brother; Don Blas Trujillo; Don Juan Vigil; Don Cornelio Vigil; Don Buenaventura Martínez; Don Charles Beaubien; and Padre Don José María Valdez. The governor emphasized:

> *It is positively known that the forces of the United States which it is announced are coming to take over this Department, are on the march and in order to consult with the most influential sons of the country as to the means we should take for our defense, I instruct you within three days after receipt of this message to present yourself before me bringing with you those citizens named in the list attached who under no pretext will be excused for we are to discuss the welfare of the Department or of its lost cause which should interest all of us.*

> *God and Liberty!*
> *Manuel Armijo*

On August 8, 1846, the governor and commandant general of New Mexico sent out an appeal to all New Mexicans, imploring them to take up arms against American forces with the purpose of defeating the Americans in battle.

The Conscript's departure

The Soldier's return

Lith. of Sarony & Major.

JEANNETTE & JEANNOT.

WORDS BY

MUSIC BY

CHARLES JEFFERYS.

CHARLES W. GLOVER.

NEW YORK
Published by ATWILL, 201, Broadway
Wm HALL & SON 239 BROADWAY C^{er} OF PARK PLACE.
FIRTH, POND & Co 1 FRANKLIN SQ.

Combat and war were glorified in song and melody. The courage of fallen soldiers was elevated. In "Jeannette & Jeannot," a girl is left behind. *Author's collection.*

A unit of French volunteers dubbed the Laclede Rangers was mustered out of St. Louis. They were named after French trader and trapper Pierre Laclede, who was one of the early founders of St. Louis. Editors of the *St. Louis Reveille* wrote the following from Fort Leavenworth on June 15, 1846: "The whole country in this region is vocal with conversation on one topic—The Santa Fe Expedition. In addition to those who have actually

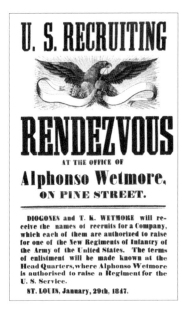

U. S. RECRUITING

RENDEZVOUS

AT THE OFFICE OF

Alphonso Wetmore,

ON PINE STREET.

DIOGENES and T. K. WETMORE will receive the names of recruits for a Company, which each of them are authorized to raise for one of the New Regiments of Infantry of the Army of the United States. The terms of enlistment will be made known at the Head Quarters, where Alphonso Wetmore is authorised to raise a Regiment for the U. S. Service.

ST. LOUIS, January, 29th, 1847.

Posters in the state of Missouri and other states touted the vast rewards of fighting a war in Mexico. Land and wealth were promised. *Author's collection.*

volunteered, there is a large number who would consent to serve as Colonels, Lieutenant Colonels, etc....The truth is, the expedition is quite a windfall to this section of the country."

A lieutenant in the U.S. regular army dragoons was assigned to rapidly train the new officers and troops of the two-hundred-plus Laclede Rangers to have them combat ready in one month. Once in New Mexico, the Rangers were involved in several battles. Captain Thomas B. Hudson of the Laclede Rangers wrote, "Yes, we shall knock at the gates of Santa Fe, as Ethan Allen knocked at the gates of Ticonderoga, and the question, 'Who is there' we shall reply, 'Open these gates in the name of the great Jehovah and the Laclede Rangers!'"

The Mormon Battalion

The state of Missouri had a serious problem. There were too many members of the Church of Latter-day Saints moving in. In his *Journal of a Santa Fe Trader*, Josiah Gregg wrote,

> *Prior to 1833, the Mormons, who were then flocking in great swarms to this favored region, had made considerable purchases of lots and tracts of land both in the town of Independence and the adjacent country...the new-comers...drew upon themselves much animadversion in consequence of the immorality of their lives...still they continued to spread and multiply, not by conversion but by immigration, to an alarming extent; and in proportion as they grew strong in numbers, they also became more exacting and bold in their pretensions...the old settlers could not think of bringing up their families in the midst of such a corrupt state of society as the Mormons were establishing....Governor Boggs deemed it necessary to order a large force of state militia to subject them....It seems very clear then, that fanatical*

delusion is not the only sin which stamps the conduct of these people with so much obliquity, or they would certainly have found permanent friends somewhere; whereas it is well known that a general aversion has prevailed against them wherever they have sojourned…it may be proper to remark, that the Mormons have invariably refused to sell any of the property they had acquired in Missouri.

The end result of antagonism against the influx of Mormon immigrants into Missouri was the Hawn's Mill Massacre. Opposition to Joseph Smith, who opposed slavery, and his Mormons was immediate and deadly. It took place on October 30, 1838. More than two hundred Missouri militiamen attacked the peaceful village of Hawn's Mill, located in Caldwell County, Missouri. They caught the settlers off guard. The militiamen fired randomly at the Mormon men and their fleeing families. After the bloody assault, around seventeen Mormon men lay dead, and many more were wounded. Missouri soldiers sexually assaulted Mormon women. Other Mormon men, women and children hid in the woods or caves. Missouri governor Lilburn W. Boggs had four days earlier issued Missouri Executive Order 44, on October 27, 1838. This has been called the "Mormon Extermination Order." Governor Boggs stated that "the Mormons must be treated as enemies, and must be exterminated or driven from the State if necessary for the public peace." As directed by Governor Boggs, General John B. Clark and his four hundred mounted troops violently attacked Mormon settlements. The governor also directed Major General David Willock to raise five hundred men and march to the northern part of the state, uniting with General Alexander Doniphan's army of five hundred to intercept any retreating Mormons. He also ordered Brigadier General Hiram G. Parks and his force of four hundred men to be in readiness.

MOVEMENT IN MISSOURI

Anti-Mormon vigilantes laid siege to the Mormon town of Dewitt by blocking all foodstuffs into the settlement in an attempt to starve the residents. The Mormons surrendered and fled. A Mormon army retaliated and fought, burning the towns of Gallatin and Millport. Mormons also fought off a militia unit in an area called Crooked Valley. Violence among civilians erupted further on both sides, and chaos reigned supreme in Missouri.

General Clark cautioned the Mormons, "You need not expect any mercy, but extermination, for I am determined the governor's orders be executed. As for your leaders, do not think, do not imagine for a moment, do not let it enter into your mind, that they will be delivered and restored to you again, for their fate is fixed, their die is cast, their doom is sealed."

Religious persecution of the Mormons in Missouri, along with no redress from the government of the United States, led to their move to Indian lands in Iowa. President Polk, through the influence of and recommendations from political leaders, decided on complete Mormon removal from American territory. It was assumed that allowing them to volunteer to fight in the Mexican-American War would take care of the Mormon problem. Joseph Smith, a prophet of the Mormon Church, had run for president in 1844. In Ohio, he had been tarred and feathered; several times in his career, he had barely escaped with his life. In his platform, Smith advocated the gradual elimination of slavery in the United States, and criminal action against political leaders who interfered with the civil rights and liberties of American citizens. He wrote, "I would not have suffered my name to have been used by my friends on any wise as President of the United States, or candidate for that office, if I and my friends could have had the privilege of enjoying our religious and civil rights as American citizens, even those rights which the Constitution guarantees unto all her citizens alike."

Joseph Smith was the first presidential candidate in American history to be assassinated. Smith had been expected to carry the election. James Knox Polk won.

TROOPS ARE MUSTERED

Colonel Stephen Watts Kearny was ordered to muster a Mormon army to help in the invasion of New Mexico. Mormon leaders were suspicious at first but then conceded. They would be allowed to wear civilian clothing while in service. Women and children could join in the march west. Forty-two dollars would be paid to each recruit. Church leaders then felt that with money provided by the government, they could purchase wagons and teams plus food and whatever they would need for Mormon families to emigrate west into Mexican territory and resettle. Brigham Young wrote, "There is war between Mexico and the United States, to whom California

Colonel Stephen W. Kearny led
Missouri troops in a conquest of
the West. *Author's collection.*

must fall prey, and if we are the first settlers the old citizens cannot have a
Hancock or Missouri pretext to mob the Saints. The thing is from above
for our own good."

The Mormon families—which included men, women, and children
touted as a "Mormon Battalion," would serve as a vanguard in the conquest
of New Mexico. The hostile expedition was underway.

BLOODLESS CONQUEST TURNS BLOODY

Military intelligence was arriving continuously from Mexico into New Mexico. Unknown to Governor Manuel Armijo, informants living in the territory—such as Charles Beaubien, Manuel Alvarez and James Magoffin, plus others involved in a clandestine inner circle—were supplying information about military operations to the United States. This conclave of individuals was holding secret meetings in Santa Fe. Fear and anxiety spread throughout the Republic of Mexico. This prompted President Antonio López de Santa Anna to issue a call to arms on April 20, 1846, from his military headquarters at Matamoros,

> Soldiers!—you have enlisted in time of peace to serve in that army for a specific term; but your obligation never implied that you were bound to violate the laws of God, and the most sacred rights of friends; the United States Government, contrary to the wishes of a majority of all honest and honorable Americans, have ordered you to take forcible possession of the territory of a friendly neighbor, who has never given her consent to such occupation. In other words, while the treaty of peace and commerce between Mexico and the United States is in full force, the United States, presuming on her strength and prosperity, and our supposed imbecility and cowardice, attempts to make you the blind instrument of her unholy and mad ambition, and forces you to appear as the hateful robbers of our dear homes, and the unprovoked violators of our dearest feelings as men and patriots.

REVISTA OFICIAL
PERIODICO DEL GOBIERNO
DEL DEPARTAMENTO DE CHIHUAHUA.

Las suscriciones las recibe en esta Capital la imprenta, en las demas poblaciones del Departamento, los secretarios de los Sres. Prefectos, los Sub-prefectos y jueces de paz respetivos, en Durango la Administracion principal de rentas y oportunamente se avisará quienes la reciben fuera de el. Su precio es el de nueve reales adelantados por trimestre para los de adentro, y doce reales franco de porte, para las de fuera de la Capital.

TOM 2. — MARTES 10 DE DICIEMBRE DE 1844. N. 50.

ASAMBLEA DEPARTAMENTAL

El ciudadano J. Mariano Monterde, General de brigada graduado, Gobernador y Comandante general del Departamento de Chihuahua, á todos sus habitantes sabed: que la Exma. Asamblea Departamental ha decretado lo que sigue.

La Asamblea Departamental de Chihuahua en uso de la facultad que le concede el art. 134 de las bases en su parte 14. ª, ha decretado lo siguiente.

Art l ° Los Ministros suplentes de que habla el art. 3. ° del decreto de 13 de Junio del presente año espedido por esta Asamblea, se aumentarán hasta el numero de seis.

2. ° Dichos suplentes tendrán las mismas cualidades y circunstancias prevenidas en el mismo decreto para los otros ministros.

3. ° El Gobierno á la mayor brevedad, hará el nombramiento respectivo.

Chihuahua Noviembre 4 de 1844.— *Luis Zuloaga*, P.—*Juan Negrete*, Srio.

Por tanto, mando se imprima, publique, circule y se cumpla en todas sus partes. Palacio del Gobierno Chihuahua Noviembre 12 de 1844.— *J Mariano Monterde.*—*Felix de Jesus Porras*, Srio.

El ciudadano J. Mariano Monterde, General de brigada graduado, Gobernador y Comandante general del Departamento de Chihuahua, á todos sus habitantes sabed: que la Exma. Asamblea Departamental, ha decretado lo que sigue.

La Asamblea Departamental de Chihuahua ha tenido á bien decretar.

1. ° La oficina principal encargada de la recaudacion del arbitrio establecido por la ley de 7 de Agosto del presente año, formará y remitirá mensalmente á la pagaduria Departamental un escrupuloso corte de caja de lo que haya producido en el Departamento el espresado arbitrio, individualizando los enteros físicos y los virtuales y los puntos en donde quede alguna ecsistencia.

2. ° La pagaduria formará igualmente cada mes un estado demostrativo de la distribucion que haya dado á los productos del mes anterior, y remitirá al Gobierno uno y otro documento para que publicados por medio del periodico oficial, se satisfaga el público de la legal inversion que ha tenido el espresado arbitrio.

3. ° Cada mes se dará á los empleados la paga que les corresponde, mas si los productos no fuesen bastantes se les distribuirá no obstante lo que se reuniere bajo el mas equitativo prorrateo.

Chihuahua Noviembre 28 de 1844.— *Luis Zuloaga.*—*Juan Negrete*, Srio.

Por tanto, mando se imprima publique, circule y se cumpla en todas sus partes. Palacio del Gobierno Chihuahua Diciembre 5 de 1844.— *J. Mariano Monterde.*—*Felix de Jesus Porras*, Srio.

ARANCEL

á que deben arreglarse en el Departamento para el cobro de sus honorarios y derechos judiciales, los jueces de primera instancia, escribanos, procuradores de numero y demas curiales ó personas que puedan intervenir en los juicios.

(Continúa.)

CAPITULO SESTO.

Del tasador de costas

Art. 1. ° Por los procesos ó cualquiera especie de diligencia que se hubieren de tazar, llevará el que ejerce es el encargo á seis granos por cada foja las que reconociere para hacer la regulacion: en el concepto de que por corto que sea el numero de fojas no han de bajar sus derechos de un peso.

2. ° A mas de la vista cobrará un peso por cada pliego de los que contenga la tasacion y el costo del papel.

CAPITULO SETIMO,

De los Ministros ejecutores y comisarios.

Art. 1. ° Los Ministros ejecutores por las posesiones, embargos y lanzamientos

que hicieren, concluyendose en una diligencia, lleva án dos ps. dos rs., y si se repitieren estas por ser numerosos los bienes y no pederse feneser en una diligencia llevarán igual cantidad por cada mañana ó tarde que invirtieren, si la diligencia se practicare fuera del lugar del juicio, á mas de los derechos cobrarán a razon de un peso por legua de ida y vuelta.

2. ° De las comisiones ordinarias que se les cometieren en virtud de mandamiento, llevarán un peso, y siendo dentro de la ciudad y sus barrios, saliendo fuera dos ps. y ademas uno por cada legua que anduvieren de ida y vuelta.

3. ° Por la cobranza de autos, teniendo efecto la devolucion á la oficina, llevarán seis rs. que cobrarán de la parte por quien se acuse la rebeldia y si se hubiere dificultado la saca de los autos por que se ocultase el responsable ó hubiese habido apremio, cobrarán á razon de un peso por cada mañana ó tarde que invierten.

4. ° Los Ministros de vara ó comisarios por cada orden de comprehendo vervad ó por escrito que lleven á las partes, dos rs., si fuere dentro del lugar, y cuatro si fuere en los suburbios.

CAPITULO OCTAVO

De las demas personas que puedan intervenir en los juicios

De los contadores partidores de herencias

Art 1. ° Los contadores partidóres de herencias por el examen de todos los documentos é instrucciones, formacion de cuentas de division y particion del caudal hereditario, cobrarán por razon de derechos el cinco por ciento de su importe cuando pasare de cien ps. y no esceda de mil. Si pasare de esta cantidad pero no de la de diez mil, llevarán á mas de los derechos anteriores: doce rs, por ciento de diez mil pesos. Cuando el importe del caudal pase de diez mil ps. y no de cincuenta mil, cobrará á mas de los derechos antecedentes seis rs. por ciento de la cantidad que exceda de diez mil pesos. Pasando el caudal de cincuenta mil y no de cien mil, llevarán tres rs. por ciento de la cantidad que exceda de dichos cincuenta mil ps á mas de los derechos regulados anteriormente· Y si el

An issue of *La Revista Oficial, Periódico del Gobierno, del Departamento de Chihuahua*. The official military newspaper provided Governor Armijo with news of American activities. *Author's collection.*

Such villainy and outrage, I know, is perfectly repugnant to the noble sentiments of any gentleman, and it is base and foul to rush you on to certain death, in order to aggrandize a few lawless individuals, in defiance of the laws of God and man! It is to no purpose if they tell you that the law for the annexation of Texas justifies your occupation of the Rio Bravo del Norte; for by this act they rob us of a great part of Tamaulipas, Coahuila, Chihuahua, and New Mexico.

Colonel Stephen Watts Kearney, colonel of the First Dragoons, headquarters of the Army of the West, camped on the Arkansas River at Bent's Fort, wrote to Governor and Commanding General Manuel Armijo of New Mexico on August 1, 1846: "Sir: By the annexation of Texas to the United States, the Rio Grande from its mouth to its source forms at this time the Boundary between her and Mexico, and I come by orders of the government to take possession of the Country, over a part of which you are now presiding as Governor."

Once Manuel Armijo knew about the intentions of Kearny and the forces he led, Armijo prepared to engage the enemy. Approximately five thousand New Mexican troops were recruited. Armijo instructed Colonel Diego Archuleta to set up fortifications in an area called Apache Pass (or Canyon). The governor remained in Santa Fe, completing arrangements before joining his forces. During this period, Archuleta took it upon himself to disband the troops and told them to return to their homes. By the time Armijo showed up with a force of around two hundred regular troops, he was appalled by what he discovered. Here, the story is mired in legend and confusion. Some say Armijo decided not to fight so as to avoid unnecessary loss of life. Also written is that Archuleta said the volunteers and officers did not wish to fight, so they simply went home. Other myths claim General Armijo was a coward and fled the scene to save his own skin. Regardless of the truth concerning events, Armijo was unexpectedly left without an army to defend New Mexico from what was to transpire. Americans were overjoyed with an apparent "Bloodless Conquest" of New Mexico.

The American Flag Is Raised

In August 1846, Colonel Stephen Watts Kearny and his Missouri volunteers raised the American flag over the Palace of the Governors in Santa Fe. Kearny set himself up as the head of a temporary government and immediately went about establishing a set of laws to govern the territory. He appointed Colonel Alexander William Doniphan and Willard P. Hall to draw up a document, which would be released to the citizens of New Mexico, outlining how they would be governed by the American military and civilian government. Both men used parts of the laws of the Republic of Texas and Missouri statutes to produce what would be known as the Kearny Code. The code exceeded one hundred pages. Five hundred copies were printed, two columns to a page, using Bodoni roman type. Most historians agree the code was printed on a press owned by a Taos priest, Padre Don Antonio José Martínez, which he had brought to New Mexico in 1835. He used this press to print his church missals, textbooks for a school and seminary he had established in Taos and a newspaper he called *El Crepúsculo de la Libertad* (*The Dawn of Liberty*). It is believed the priest loaned the press to Kearny.

Of special note is that any New Mexican who did not follow the rule of law or his or her duty to the new government could have personal property and lands confiscated. Contrary to Spanish and later Mexican law, under which women could own land and inherit and transfer homes and land to

A drawing by American Missourian soldier E.C. shows Mexican soldiers and a priest circa 1846. Governor Manuel Armijo is depicted as a fat pear on a plate. *Author's collection.*

Kearny and his troops suffered a defeat and were wounded at the Battle of San Pascual in California. He and his soldiers were riding mules. *Author's collection.*

others, under American law, women were not allowed to own homes or land. A section of the Kearny Code called "Crimes and Punishment" delineated punishments for felonies and misdemeanors. These included lashings on bare backs with a whip, including for women. Those dispensing this punishment did not hesitate in being harsh. The severity of the number of whippings, or floggings, depended on the crime committed and the judges imposing the law. Those convicted of breaking the laws were imprisoned for a length of time ranging from two to ten or more years, depending on the crime committed, and they faced hard physical labor. Castration for rape could be invoked as well as the death penalty in cases of burglary or robbery. Prisoners were held securely by handcuffs, chains and blocks and were also shackled. Anyone peddling goods in the territory was levied a heavy tax, depending on whether the person was peddling on foot, by using a beast of burden, or carriage, cart or wagon.

Self-proclaimed governor of New Mexico Stephen Watts Kearny admitted to close friend Susan Shelby Magoffin that in giving reassurance to the local populace, as she wrote in her journal, "He paraded through some little village in the priests procession, carrying as did all of his officers a lighted candle lightening the train of the Virgin Mary making a fool of himself."

NEW MEXICO MILITARY DISTRICTS

Unbeknownst to Colonel Kearny and other Americans was that the New Mexico Territory, since it was so vast, had been divided under Mexico into separate military districts that included what are now parts of Colorado. These districts were established according to a Republic of Mexico congressional resolution, Division of the Department following the 134th Article. The Department of New Mexico was divided into three districts, which were called Central, North and Southeast. Each district was divided into seven counties, and these into three municipalities. "The population, according to the statistics, which are presented for this purpose, is 100,064. The capital of the department is Santa Fe." Brigadier General Mariano Martínez de Lejanza, constitutional governor of the Department of New Mexico, enforced the division of these separate military districts with counties and capitals through a June 17, 1844 decree issued by President Jesús María Gallegos. The Division of the Department following the 134th Article was as follows, according to Benjamin Read in his book *Guerra México Americana*:

Central District

Article 2. This district is hereby divided into three counties, which shall be called Santa Fe, Santa Ana, and San Miguel del Bado. The capital of these three counties shall be the city of Santa Fe.

Article 3. The first county shall comprise all the inhabitant of Santa Fe, San Ildefonso, Pojoaque, Nambe, Cuyamungue, Tesuque, Rio Tesuque, Cienega, Cieneguilla, Agua Fria, Galisteo, El Real del Oro, and Tuerto. The county seat is Santa Fe. The number of inhabitants is 12,500.

Article 4. The second county shall comprise the inhabitants of Rayado, Cochiti, Peña Blanca, Chillili, Santo Domingo, Cubero, San Felipe, Jemez, Silla, Santa Ana, Angostura, and Algodones. The number of inhabitants is 10,500. The county seat is fixed at Algodones.

Article 5. The third county shall comprise the inhabitants of Pecos, Gusano, Rio de la Vaca, Mula, Estramos, San José, San Miguel del Bado, Pueblo, Puertecito, Cuesta, Cerrito, Anton Chico, Tecolote, Las Vegas, and Sapello. Inhabitants, 18,800; county shall be San Miguel.

Provincial tricolor, the yellow, white and red flag of New Mexico, circa 1840. Yellow, white and red banners flank a stylized Mexican eagle. *Author's collection.*

Northern District

Article 6. This district is divided into two counties, called Rio Arriba and Taos. The capital is Los Luceros.

Article 7. The county of Rio Arriba comprises the inhabitants of Santa Cruz de la Cañada, Chimayo, Cañada, Truchas, Santa Clara, Vegas, Chama, Cuchillo, Abiquiú, Rio Colorado, Ojo Calient, Ranchitos, Chamita, San Juan, Rio Arriba, La Joya, and Embudo. The county seat is Los Luceros. The number of inhabitants is 15,000.

Article 8. The county of Taos comprises the inhabitants of Don Fernández, San Francisco, Arroyo Hondo, Arroyo Seco, Desmontes, Cieneguilla, Picures, Santa Bárbara, Zampas, Chamizal, Llano, Peñasco, Mora, Huérfano, and Cimarrón. The county seat is Don Fernández. The number of inhabitants amounts to 14,200.

Southeastern District

Article 9. This district is divided into two counties, called Valencia and Bernalillo. The capital is Valencia.

Article 10. The county of Valencia comprises, Valencia, San Fernando, Tomé, Socorro, Limitar, Polvaderas, Sabinal, Elames, Casa Colorada, Cebolleta, Sabino, Parida, Luis López, Belen, Los Lunas, Los Lentes, Zuni, Acoma, and El Rito. County seat, Valencia. Number of inhabitants, 20,000.

Article 11. The county of Bernalillo comprises, Isleta, Los Padillas, Pajarito, Ranchos de Atrisco, Atrisco, Palareres, Albuquerque, Alameda, Corrales, Sandia, and Bernalillo. County seat Bernalillo. Number of inhabitants, 8,204. The whole number of inhabitants of the district, 28,204.

A Troubled Takeover

Tensions in New Mexico immediately rose up. There were foreign American militants from Missouri causing problems. American control and power, which was never fully accepted by the inhabitants, was shrinking due to mistrust and difficulties involving languages. Kearny appointed a civilian government led by merchant Charles Bent and then quickly traveled with a large force to take over California. The Mormon families accompanied him. Kearny was commissioned as a brigadier general due to his success in New Mexico. He left Colonel Sterling Price with what he felt was an adequate number of soldiers to control New Mexico militarily. The American soldiers took excessive liberties, drank freely and taunted the civilians. New Mexicans felt their children would be left without hope—or a future. It began to be

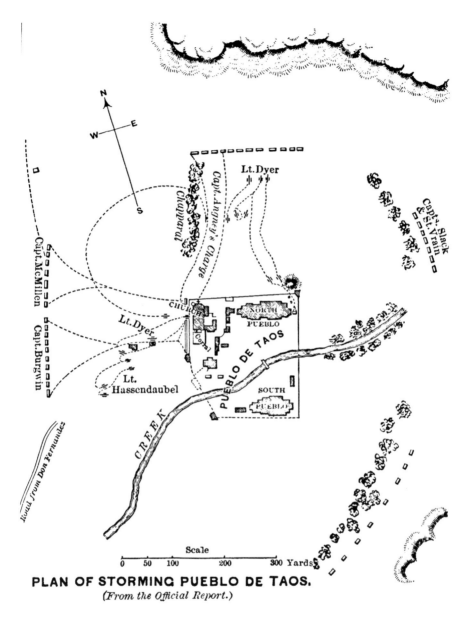

PLAN OF STORMING PUEBLO DE TAOS.
(From the Official Report.)

Plan for storming and Battle of Taos Pueblo, January 19, 1847. *Courtesy New Mexico Historical Society.*

popularly felt among New Mexicans that the only option was to attack and force the intruders out of the territory. Mexican officers began to form coalitions of Indian and New Mexican troops. Charles Bent, the unelected governor, wrote, "As other occupation troops have done at other times and places have done, they undertook to act like conquerors...these outrages are becoming so frequent that I apprehend serious consequences must result sooner or later if measures are not taken to prevent them."

In the annals of writing and recording history, it is very fortunate there are archival materials, diaries, letters and personal recollections and memoirs. Once in a while, a treasure previously unknown is unearthed. Such is the case with a document written by a member of Padre Don Antonio José Martínez's family who interviewed witnesses and recorded his own personal details of the Battle of Taos between American forces and Taos Pueblo Indians during the Mexican-American War.

Sometime near the end of the nineteenth century, Don Miguel Martínez y Santistevan—the son of Civil War first lieutenant (and later captain of the Third New Mexico Mounted Infantry and Battalion Adjunct) Inocencio Martínez wrote a firsthand account in Spanish about events that took place in Taos, New Mexico, in 1847. Inocencio Martínez was the son of Santiago Martínez, the brother of the famous Padre Antonio José Martínez. Inocencio's uncle was Colonel Pascual Bailón Martínez of the New Mexico/Mexican forces during the war with the United States. Don Miguel called himself "El Anciano de Taos" (the Old One of Taos). Don Miguel's father, Inocencio, saw action at the Battle of Glorieta, the so-called Gettysburg of the West, against the Confederates. Translated from the Spanish by author Ray John de Aragón, Miguel Martínez's account differs from American accounts and official U.S. government records; Miguel Martínez included lengthy recollections and anecdotes. Parts of eyewitness accounts in his handwritten recollections (from the author's collection) follow in *War Drums—the Battle of Taos.*

The Revolution of Taos, 1847...Up until now, there have been many writers who have given accounts of the disturbances and what precipitated those horrible times that stain the pages of the history of Taos County. Blood and sacking, everything, serves to provide a true account, without exaggeration, of the adverse spirit that arose...

The Indians of the pueblos in what we now call New Mexico resisted any invasion of their lands...they considered their territories to be their legitimate patrimony without regard, nor knowledge of the power of the

Above: Taos Pueblo, by William Henry
Jackson, unknown date. Taos Indians
revolted against American forces, and the
"Taos Massacre," in which Indian families
were killed, resulted. *Author's collection.*

Right: Taos merchant Charles Bent was
appointed by Kearny as governor. Taos
Pueblo Indians killed Bent on January 19,
1847. *Courtesy New Mexico Historical Society.*

nation of the United States, they watered the land with their blood, and gave up their lives....Just as soon as the American government established itself in New Mexico, peace and order was lost....They were displeased, and had no confidence in the new government. Discontent spread and grew each day.

Padre Antonio José Martínez was the most illustrious man in New Mexico. Besides his priestly vocation, he tried to spread education....He maintained that education would be the salvation of the Pueblo Indians. With his magnanimous heart and knowledge, he tried to remedy the situation for the Pueblos....[He maintained the American] government is like a burro that is led by lawyers...you should study the civil laws of the government, and learn the language of the country....

When it was close to the feast days of Christmas, and the new-year, the governor [Charles Bent] came to Taos to spend some time with his family....Messengers went out in all directions....It had been decided to make an assault on Santa Fe on the next night...but there was a Judas in their midst. That same night a member of their organization, ...told [his wife Doloritas] that there was a conspiracy to kill him [Bent] and all of the Americans on the following night....On the morning of the next day, the woman got on the road to deliver the message to the governor...."It's alright Doloritas, I don't believe anything that you're telling me. It's nothing but drunken stories, thank you," the governor responded....The governor turned his back to her and left the room....If the governor and the rest of his naïve men had given credence to the information that was revealed about the conspiracy, they would have avoided an impending catastrophe.

On the night of January 14, 1847...a large number of families had gathered at the home of Padre Martínez, pleading for sanctuary and help....The Indians are killing Governor Bent and other Americans! That same night they attacked the Taos plaza and Ranchos de Taos. In Arroyo Hondo, the Indians sacked the stores and the houses, and offices of the inhabitants. They reunited at the pueblo during the day.

Padre Martínez had information that a company of solders had arrived from Santa Fe at the Fort of the Rio Grande and he immediately sent a message to the captain with a messenger named Juan Chiquito, asking him for help. The Indians had the roads that went in and out of the plaza blocked. The messenger knew the lay of the land well. Juan Chiquito waited until nightfall so that the other Indians wouldn't see him. On hearing the news, the colonel set out with a company of troops. Most of the American soldiers had left the capital city of Santa Fe to fight the Navajo

Indians....Colonel Sterling Price with three hundred and ten soldiers was heading to join the battle, but changed directions upon hearing about what was happening in Taos.

Some of the insurgents arrived at Padre Martínez' house and gave him some news. "Greetings Father, we finished with all of the heretics." The priest answered, "You have done wrong to the government of the United States. It is very powerful. What you have done may cost you your lives."...

An Indian girl from Taos pueblo named Santanita and her husband left the pueblo, searching for help. She informed us that on that night or the following day, a great force of Indians and Spanish/Mexicans would assault the plaza, and all of the surrounding areas. When nighttime fell they sent Don Miguel Romero, who was a courageous man mounted on a mule, to prepare the people of Ranchitos so that they would be aware.... The women who were trembling from fear were attempting to hide Doña Luz Beaubien, the wife of Narcissus Beaubien, in a very large trunk, but it was decided to hide Santanita, because the Indians would consider her to be a traitor....On the morning of the 15th, they found those that were killed on the previous night....Governor Bent, Narcissus Beaubien, Louis Lee, Pablo Jaramillo, and Cornelio Vigil, along with several others were discovered.....A celebrated woman of 90 years of age talked about all of the things that happened, including anecdotes. She mentioned that after seeing the remains of Narcissus, she met up with Pedro Celestino, and José Gregorio. These were members of the revolutionaries that took an active part in the invasion that night....

On January 19th a great number of warriors went to the Taos plaza. The group was composed of Indians, and New Mexicans to form the assault. The Indian chief called Tomasito; Little Tom had distinguished himself as the hero of the revolt. He was mounted on a superb horse, and he led the force to the suburbs of the plaza....Colonel Sterling Price was closing in on the opposite side of the plaza. It was already late in the afternoon. In a place called Cruz Alta, High Cross, he discovered, with the help of a telescope, the dust kicked up in the air by the force. From there he fired a canon to try to disperse the march....

The colonel along with his troops began the march to the pueblo on the following day to test his weapons against those of the enemy who had theirs in the ramparts or exterior walls of the pueblo. He began his attack by firing at the protective walls that fortified the Taos pueblo. The soldiers firing from their camp made a futile attempt at the thick protective walls. Each day the fuselage was more furious with artillery and arms against the

The massive San Gerónimo Church at Taos Pueblo was viewed as a fortress by American troops. Painting by K.M. Chapman. *Courtesy New Mexico Historical Society.*

enemy, but it was useless....As a last recourse he ordered the troops to scale the walls, but they were all killed. Captain Burgwin had ordered cannon moved to about fifty yards of the pueblo in a desperate attempt to have his troops storm the walls, but he also lost his life in the process. Thirty or more soldiers quickly died. This motivated the Indians. This is the way the battle continued for two days without letting up. Each day, Colonel Price and his forces retreated back to the Taos plaza....The families of the warriors took refuge within the church....

On the third day of the arduous battle, that did not result in a victory for either side....A man by the name of Tomas Torrez came out of the pueblo and made arrangements for the surrender of the pueblo to the American army. American troops...gave him enough explosives....Following Price's instructions; he bore a hole into a wall of the church and threw the explosives inside. With the resulting explosion, the families that were taking refuge inside came out running. The soldiers fired at the families, killing many of the men, women, and children. The church of San Geronimo was totally destroyed by canon balls, and firing. The insurgents then gave up and surrendered by raising a white flag. The colonel shackled many of the insurgents...and executed all of the leaders by hanging, to make an example of them to others. He executed the pueblo Indian governor and General Pablo Montoya, an officer of the Mexican army whom he had captured and detained. He also executed a sixteen-year old Indian boy named Coloradito Sandoval, who was from a good family....

Colonel Sterling Price commanded the Second Regiment of Missouri volunteers. He served as a Confederate major general in the Civil War. *Courtesy New Mexico Historical Society.*

The government of the United States continued in power over this vast territory. The inhabitants in general submitted to the new government…the Latino race of New Mexico suffered, and they were considered a conquered people by both civil and ecclesiastical American authorities. We were strangers in our own land.

Colonel Sterling Price, commanding the Army of New Mexico, wrote in his report to the adjutant general of the U.S. Army in Washington, D.C., on February 15, 1847, about events in Taos:

The Pueblos of Taos were accounted the most warlike and the bravest race in Mexico; certainly the circumstances of the murder of Governor Bent on the 19th, evince their extreme barbarity.…The fate of Mr. Leal, the district-attorney, was still more horrible, for they murdered him with all the refinement of savage barbarity. They shot arrows into his body for some time, not sufficiently deep to destroy his life, and, after that, they shot them into his face and eyes, and then scalped him alive. After torturing him thus for a long time, they finally dispatched him and threw his body into the street.

On January 20, 1847, a Santa Fe presidio commander named Jesús Tafoya sent out a military directive to all officers of New Mexico militia and regular troops. He called for all to mobilize immediately. The government of the United States had declared war against Mexico. In isolated New Mexico, news certainly did not travel fast. Spanish settlements were far apart, and people during this period were more concerned with the struggles of living and fighting off marauding Indians that were a constant source of consternation. However, when called upon, its inhabitants were indeed prepared to defend New Mexico. Colonel Diego Archúleta had also disbanded the forces and had assured them that it was not necessary to take threats of a takeover seriously. Supported by Don Pedro Vigil and also signed by Juan Bautista Vigil y Mares, secretary, Mariano Martínez and José Félix Jubia, secretary, Juan Antonio Garcia's directive read:

> *To the Defenders of Their Country: With the end to shake off the yoke bound on us by a foreign government, and as your Military Inspector General appointed by the Legitimate Commander for the Supreme Government of Mexico, which we proclaim in favor of: The moment you receive this communication, you will place in readiness all the companies under your command, keeping them ready for the 22nd day of this month, so that the forces may be, on the day mentioned, at that point. Take the*

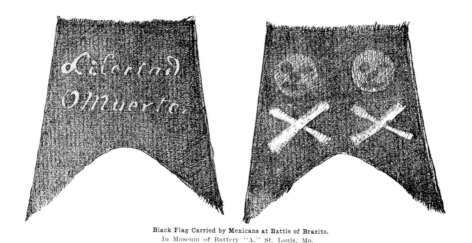

Black Flag Carried by Mexicans at Battle of Brazito.
In Museum of Battery "A," St. Louis, Mo.

New Mexico "Liberty or Death" battle flag. Skull and crossbones meant victory or death to the New Mexico forces. *Courtesy New Mexico Historical Society.*

*precaution to observe if the forces of the enemy advance any toward these
points, and if it should so happen, appoint a courier and dispatch him
immediately so that exertions may be doubled, understanding that there
must not be resistance or delay in giving the answer to the bearer of this
official document.*

*By the order of the Inspector of Arms, Don Antonio María Trujillo, I
herewith send you this dispatch that the moment this comes to hand you will
raise all the forces, together with all the inhabitants that are able to bear
arms, connecting them also with persons in San Juan de Los Caballeros, by
to-morrow, counting from the 22nd day of the present month, and not later
than eight o'clock in the morning.*

*We have declared war with the Americans and it is now time that we
shall all take our arms in our hands in defense of our abandoned country.*

You are held responsible for the execution of the above order.

When the Missourians took over Santa Fe during the Mexican-American
War, the New Mexico capital was moved by New Mexican military
commanders to San Juan de Los Caballeros (the original capital of New
Mexico during the Spanish colonial period), near the city of Española. New
Mexican military officers and officials hoped to mobilize and retake Santa
Fe from Missourian/American troops.

Due to the actions of Colonel Sterling Price, commanding U.S. forces
in Santa Fe, as well as executions for treason that were taking place,
W.L. Marcy, U.S. secretary of war, sent a memorandum from the War
Department in Washington dated June 26, 1847: In the *Report of the Secretary
of War, Communication in Answer to the resolution of the Senate report and map of the
examination of New Mexico made by Lieutenant J.W. Abert of the topographical Corps.
30th Congress, First Session, Executive No. 23, Senate* is stated:

*The territory conquered by our arms does not become, by the mere act of
conquest, a permanent part of the United States, and the inhabitants of
such territory are not, to the full extent of the term, citizens of the United
States…it is not the proper use of legal terms to say that their offence was
treason committed against the United States; for, to the government of the
United States, as the government under our constitution, it would not be
correct to say they owed allegiance.…You will I trust, excuse an allusion to
another subject not officially before me: I mean the state of discipline among
our troops at Santa Fe.*

Another depiction of the Battle of Brazito between Doniphan's troops and Mexican/New Mexican forces. The battle ended in a draw. Unknown engraver and date. *Author's collection.*

Various complaints were received at the U.S. House of Representatives during the ensuing months after Kearny, now a brigadier general, entered New Mexico. U.S. representatives believed that the officers of the Army of the West had overstepped the boundaries of their authority. President Polk, in addressing these concerns about excesses of power, stated that they were "the offspring of a patriotic desire," and the end result had "resulted in no physical injury, but can and will be early corrected, in a manner to alienate as little as possible the good feelings of the inhabitants of the territory." The excesses were not corrected, but steadily increased in New Mexico and other areas of the Southwest. The Kearny Code remained in effect for twenty-plus years.

Lewis Hector Garrard, author of the 1850 book *Wah-to-yah and the Taos Trail; or Prairie Travel and Scalp Dances, with a Look at Los Rancheros from Muleback and the Rocky Mountain Campfire*, wrote an eyewitness account:

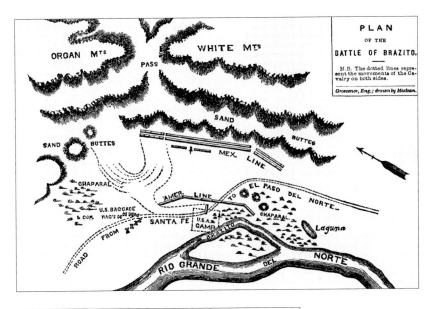

Above: Battle of Brazito Battle Plan. American numbers of casualties were officially diminished so as not to discourage troops. *Courtesy New Mexico Historical Society.*

Left: On September 6, 1848, Commander Major B. Beall, Ninth Military Department at Santa Fe, issued Special Order No. 40 safeguarding the person of Diego Archúleta. *National Archives.*

It certainly did appear to be a great assumption of the part of the Americans to conquer a country and then arraign the revolting inhabitants for treason. American judges sat on the bench, New Mexicans and Americans filled the jury box, and an American soldiery guarded the halls. Verily, a strange mixture of violence and justice—a strange middle ground between martial and common-law. After an absence of a few minutes the jury returned with a verdict, "Guilty in the first degree." Five for murder, one for treason. Treason indeed! What did the poor devil know about his new allegiance? I left the room, sick at heart. Justice! Out upon the word when its distorted meaning is a warrant for murdering those who defended to the last their country and their homes.

SLASH AND BURN

In a Mexican War correspondence series published in the *St. Louis Reveille*, Missouri soldier Richard Smith Elliot quotes Colonel Stephen Watts Kearny as saying on the morning of August 15, 1846, "As the American flag was raised, and the cannon boomed its glorious national salute from the hill…a sigh of commiseration…escaped from many a manly breast, as the wail of grief arose above the din of our horses' tread, and reached our ears from the depth of the gloomy-looking buildings on every hand."

According to Elliot, his colonel apparently knew the citizens felt deep sorrow for their misfortunes and he was apparently struck by their grief. Needless to say, Santa Feans were completely befuddled and dismayed with the American presence in their city, although it was not completely unusual for American troops to escort Santa Fe Trail caravans to the capital. In fact, it was known that a large group of American families was also on the way. Therefore, this American army detachment could, in fact, be a group of soldiers escorting the men, women and children. New Mexicans were confused, then alarmed. This unexpected appearance of American troops, as their governor had forewarned them, could actually pose a sudden danger to their lives. American conspirators had succeeded in camouflaging their treason against Mexico. James Magoffin and others convinced Colonel Diego Archuleta the intention of the United States was to take over northeastern New Mexico, including Santa Fe, Taos, Mora and Las Vegas—an area previously claimed by the Republic of Texas, which was now supposedly a part of U.S. territory through the annexation of Texas as a state. Magoffin

M1841 Mountain Howitzers, used in New Mexico against presidio soldiers and Indians. Explosive shells had a range of one thousand feet and tore the enemy to shreds. *Author's collection.*

assured Archuleta he could have everything south of this area and control it as a governor. Bewilderment spread throughout the territory like wildfire. The prospects of an actual American invasion provoked plans for immediate retaliation, especially after the rights and privileges of New Mexicans and Indians were violated. Horror ruled in New Mexico.

In his memoirs, Union Civil War captain José Rafael Sotero Chacón wrote that he and his troops fought in the famous Battle of Valverde against the Confederates, in which Chacón distinguished himself for his bravery and leadership during combat. Chacón served under Lieutenant Colonel José Francisco Chávez as captain of Company K, First Infantry. He was later commissioned as a major and commanded Fort Stanton. As a young military cadet, Chacón, along with other New Mexican cadets who were being trained at the military academy in Chihuahua, Mexico, had been prepared to fight the Americans during the Mexican-American War.

Rafael Chacón was attached to the Taos Company of militia and lived in Mora, New Mexico, from 1848 through 1849. His father was Albino Chacón, a government official serving in the administration of Governor Manuel Armijo in Santa Fe. Governor and General Armijo ordered Albino Chacón to call the New Mexico militia to report for duty to confront the

New Mexico or Bust! Horace Greeley said, "Go west, young man." He touted land, adventure and riches American adventurers could have simply for the taking. *Author's collection.*

American forces. Rafael Chacón wrote an account (translated from Spanish by the author) of what he recalled about the suffering of local citizens when American troops, after their entry into and conquest of Santa Fe, attacked local villages toward the end of 1846 and into 1847:

> *When nightfall came, my father arrived to where he left us, and he guided us through the mountains to Santa Fe. My uncle Juan Velarde had remained in Santa Fe, taking care of our home, and he had not joined the forces at Cañoncito. The next day before we got to Chimayo, one of our own arrived to leave me at my Aunt Manuela Cruz' home. She was my father's aunt, and half sister of my grandfather, Don Felipe Chacón. In November of 1846, my father arrived with all of the family to the house. A company of American dragoons had come twice to arrest him, but we were able to*

save him in the Chiquito River....American troops were advancing towards Taos in 1847 and there were some encounters with the Militia that was organized into guerillas....When the American troops advanced to Taos in two divisions, one towards Embudo, and the other to Las Trampas and El Chamizal, the people along with their families and farm animals ran away trying to escape. They all took refuge at the Cañon del Rio between Picuris, Las Trampas, and Embudo, there they suffered severely for a long time hiding among the branches of the pine trees. I remember that there was such a terror instilled by the Americans that if a dog barked they killed it. They tied the mouths of the burros so that they wouldn't bray, and they killed the roosters that crowed.

Samuel Chamberlain confessed to the slaughter and scalping of Mexican men, women and children in a cave by Captain John Joel Glanton and Texas Rangers. *Author's collection.*

Campfires were only allowed at night so that the smoke would not be detected. After the assault on Taos where the Indians fought fiercely, the Americans captured some of the Indians and Mexicans and executed them…they sent some companies of soldiers to Mora. The people ran away, and the soldiers burned the plazas, the granaries and everything that was not taken by the residents. My uncle Don Damacio Chacón, my father's brother, didn't even have mattresses for his family's use. I remember that my father-in-law who was well liked by my father, built a structure with branches, and went for our family at Chamizal so that everyone could be together during the critical times of the invasion. All of the family cared deeply about me and were in fear.

New Forms of Warfare

Military tactics have evolved through the centuries, but it was during the Mexican-American War in New Mexico that approaches specifically meant to bring a population to its knees were tried and tested. Access to food was used as a weapon, along with the burning of homes and the killing of livestock. In his book *The Conquest of California and New Mexico, by the Forces of the United States, in the Years 1846 & 1847*, James Madison Cutts, who accompanied the expedition, provides a rare glimpse as to what actually happened in the territory, written from Santa Fe on August 4, 1847:

At the destruction of the town of Los Pías, on the 6th of July last, by the troops under the command of Major Edmonson, we found letters written… giving a plan of their intended operations, and asking the citizens to be in readiness for action at a moment's warning…no doubt of being able to strike a final decisive blow.…The prisoners…stated that many of their men, had gone to the town of Loquesta to join their leader, General Gonzales. Loquesta is a town of considerable size and admirably located for defense.

The towns of Los Pías and Loquesta were destroyed. Previous to this, the town of Mora, along with nearby settlements, was razed through a scorched-earth policy. This included setting fire to cultivated fields and crops. Alfalfa fields and feed for horses and farm animals were not spared. Rich farmlands and ranches were targeted, and the horses and mules were taken. Mora's

San Gerónimo Church at Taos Pueblo destroyed. Real-Photo Postcard, circa 1907. Colonel Sterling Price ordered fleeing Indian families shot. Howitzers did the job. *Author's collection.*

population had been about two thousand, nearly all of whom took to the mountains. U.S. troops led by Captain Jesse I. Morin on February 1, 1847, then destroyed the place—with the exception of three houses occupied by invalids as well as a large quantity of grain, then much wanted by the Mexican army in New Mexico, thus unfortunately causing some horrors of war to be felt by the New Mexicans.

Food, Fire and Water Used as Weapons

The food supplies to adequately maintain the operations of the American army were minimal. In fact, when Kearny's forces entered New Mexico over what is called the Ratón Pass from Colorado, the troops were pretty well starving. They considered it a godsend when they came across a sheepherder tending a substantial flock of sheep. Kearny's forces appropriated the sheep after accusing and apprehending the sheepherder as a spy. They feasted and with renewed spirits could continue on rather than turn back to Bent's Fort.

Livestock and wild game became a means for the Americans to fight an enemy. Hundreds of buffalo were shot and left to rot. This was used as a method of bringing the Indians to the negotiating table to sign treaties, which were eventually broken out of convenience. Watering holes were also purposely contaminated. The Indians, due to the military policies of the American government in New Mexico, were forced to plunder so their families would not starve to death.

Padre Martínez wrote to President Santa Anna in 1843 that the Americans settling in different parts of the north and trading with the Indians were causing

> *The loss of millions of calves. It is easily imagined that an attack made upon a herd of buffalo cows, amounting to three or four thousand, the most part with calves…is certain that the buffaloes must greatly diminish in consequence and this constant slaughter will finally result in the extinction of the species in a very short time…and the Indians will be all the more obliged to resort to pillage and robbery.*

The Americans had decided to strike the hinterlands of New Mexico after combat such as the First Battle of Mora, on January 24, 1847, won by New Mexicans; the Second Battle of Mora, on February 1, 1847, in which the town and church serving as a refuge for families were destroyed

Second Battle of Mora, February 1, 1847. Howitzers are seen pounding the town, which was leveled. C.K. Chapman painting. *Courtesy New Mexico Historical Society.*

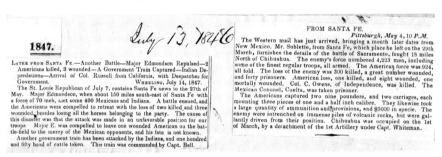

Newspaper story of the Battle of Embudo Pass, which took place on January 29, 1847. New Mexican forces were victorious. Major Edmonson's official report was contrary to what has been written. *Author's collection.*

and fleeing people wounded or killed by the firing of howitzers; the Battle of Santa Cruz de la Cañada, on January 24, 1847; the Battle of Embudo, on January 29, 1847; the Battle of Las Vegas, on July 6, 1847, in which much of the town was destroyed, including the church; and the Battle of Cienega, on July 9, 1847. The numbers of dead and wounded soldiers and civilians resulting from those actions are not officially known. Also not known is how many battles and skirmishes took place. Except for General Manuel Cortez, the names of the Mexican officers are not recorded, but the names of American commanders and leaders are.

It is not noted how many towns simply disappeared from maps. One such town was El Placer (Americanized to Placer), where gold was discovered in 1828 and which is regarded as the first recorded site of gold mining in the United States west of the Mississippi River. Gold-hungry Americans inundated the town of El Placer in 1847, prior to the California Gold Rush. After the Mexican-American War, the town was gone, along with its original inhabitants. Other New Mexico towns, such as El Tuerto, San Pedro, Manzano, Loma Parda, San Rafael, Trementina, Cabezón, Hermosa, Santa Rita (where copper had been mined since Spanish colonial days), Pinos Altos, Alma, Mogollón, Valedon and many others, also disappeared. Los Valles was erased from existence on July 6, 1847. Every building in the village was destroyed. No one today knows what happened to the residents.

8

DIVIDE AND CONQUER

Through its Missourian volunteers, the United States used classic examples of military techniques and strategies to defeat New Mexico during the Mexican-American War. The American War Department created new approaches to the task of conquering New Mexico due to the defeats of Republic of Texas forces during their attempted invasions. Fifty thousand dollars (a considerable amount of money) was given to James Magoffin to bribe officials and undermine military operations, and Magoffin was given a free hand as to how to expend these funds to be the most advantageous to coerce officials. Division among the populace was stimulated through payoffs and the promise of important positions in the new government. This fostered cooperation with the Americans by some New Mexicans, but it also established mistrust among those who were still patriotic to the Mexican Republic. Economics entered into the framework with the deterioration of trade and commerce on the Santa Fe Trail.

New Mexicans were torn between allegiance to their country or the possibilities of new opportunities under another government. What proved to be of the most value to the Americans, albeit temporarily, was the use of deception to gain leverage. Separating forces into two groups and sending approximately five hundred Mormon families—with men dressed in regular farming clothes and women with children and infants—onto the Santa Fe Trail very effectively created confusion. This also helped to divide thoughts among Mexican forces. Some were bent on fighting, while others did not want to attack pioneering families on their way to California. War

Battle of Embudo, unknown engraver and date. Residents chipped crosses into rocks where family died. Major Edmonson's troops later attacked the town. *Author's collection.*

A promissory note from Forcarea Biniva dated January 12, 1849, to Allaire and Overman, for twenty dollars and fifty cents. The two men became lenders. *Author's collection.*

materials ordered by Governor and General Armijo were cut off since American spies living in Santa Fe provided their compatriots with detailed information as to shipments of goods traveling through the Santa Fe Trail and other areas. Armijo, because a trusted officer disbanded his army, journeyed and reported himself to the Mexican military command center in Chihuahua, Mexico. General Armijo was tried for treason, but he was fully exonerated after the facts were revealed. Fully documented evidence to this effect strangely disappeared at some point. Armijo then planned to mount a counteroffensive with new troops and retake the capital of Santa Fe, but his plans were impeded by a massive American attack on Mexico. After some time, the beaten, dejected general returned to his homeland, where he was humiliated with printed words by American writers. He was totally disillusioned.

Armijo had experienced an overwhelming victory over the Texans. This time, a victory over the Americans would have ensured his legacy for posterity. This escaped his grasp.

NEW MEXICO OCCUPATION AND RESISTANCE

Once American forces entered Santa Fe in August 1846, the Mexican provincial capital was moved to Santa Cruz de La Cañada, a heavily fortified town with a substantial number of soldiers. The original, early Spanish colonial capital at San Juan de Los Caballeros became another important military base of operations for New Mexicans and Pueblo Indians. For all intents and purposes, Santa Cruz became a temporary capital until which time Santa Fe could be retaken. The Americans immediately began construction of Fort Marcy, named after the secretary of war, and mounted cannon at strategic points. New Mexicans regrouped and, with Indian allies, attacked various locations. The American military immediately went into a war of attrition by stymieing food and supplies and worked to erode resources in New Mexico. Americans were receiving continuous shipments of supplies and munitions from Missouri. These shipments included additional howitzers.

American forces began raiding towns and villages where it was believed there could be resistance to the American government at Santa Fe. They intended to separate insurgents so it would be easier to defeat the enemy troops. For New Mexicans, dwindling supplies became a logistical nightmare, especially when scorched-earth tactics were used by the American military. Fighting on multiple fronts then began. The American military was successful in discovering the weakest groups and overwhelmed them by destroying the centers of operation, which were the actual villages.

Counteroffensives were begun by General Manuel Cortez and his battalion. After he saw the devastation of his town of Mora and nearby villages, Cortez became very actively involved and quickly mounted an elite

Battle of Las Vegas, July 6, 1847. Major Edmonson used a howitzer to level a church and buildings. K.M. Chapman painting. *Courtesy New Mexico Historical Society.*

force to attack American troops. He began a series of protracted probing and harassing attacks in different locations. His troop movements at times went undetected; and when in actual battle, his forces were involved in false retreats after fighting the Americans in the impassable terrain of mountains and water. In some cases, combat was at close quarters. In time, the back of the resistance to American rule was broken through the constant use of howitzers that were targeted indiscriminately on Mexicans and their Indian allies.

General Manuel Cortez won some battles and skirmishes with the Americans, including the major Battle of Red River Canyon, fought from May 26 to 27, 1847. After the war, he became a hunted man. Rewards for his capture or death were offered. In official reports of the ongoing skirmishes with Cortez and his forces, the Americans lowered the numbers of their wounded and killed so as not to discourage U.S. troops in New Mexico. It was also the American practice to increase the reported numbers of the dead and wounded of the enemy. But General Cortez employed guerilla tactics, and he could not be tracked down. He and his troops simply fought and then disappeared. The American military believed General Cortez and his men had gone into the Staked Plains, an area of arid land spreading out for hundreds of miles from New Mexico into Texas. They went out on a fruitless search.

Torreon at Manzano. The circular torreones were defensive towers meant to protect the people from the enemy. American howitzers would finally bring them down. *Author's collection.*

Battle of Brazito, December 25, 1846. Colonel Alexander Doniphan led Missouri troops. New Mexican forces retreated after Major Antonio Ponce de León was wounded. *Author's collection.*

A rare lengthy ballad about Cortez recounting Cortez's fate offers a glimpse into his story. Only a few stanzas are presented here, to illustrate what became of him according to legend. The second half of the ballad has never been found. The story goes that Cortez traveled to Chihuahua, Mexico, and faded into the crowds for years while a manhunt continued unabated.

> *"El Corrido de Manuel Cortez" (The Ballad of Manuel Cortez)*
> *by Miguel Martínez y Santistevan, "El Anciano de Taos" (the Old One*
> *of Taos)*

> *1st. July 10ᵗʰ of 1884*
> *When the event took place*
> *At night in one act*
> *The disgrace began.*
> *2nd. Two men are injured,*
> *And it is not known why.*
> *One is Luciano Trujillo,*
> *And the other is Manuel Cortez.*
> *3rd. In the Villa of Chihuahua,*
> *They began to live,*
> *And at one in the morning,*
> *They got together with Valdez.*
> *4th. Sotelo jumped violently,*
> *With a pistol in his hand,*
> *And those who were inside,*
> *He was threatening.*
> *5th. When they went outside,*
> *They invited Cortez,*
> *They spoke gross words.*
> *Pronounced in English.*
> *6th. From inside came out Luciano,*
> *And they tangled up outside,*
> *This is what Cruz de Herrera says,*
> *Two shots were fired.*
> *7th. Sotelo fired and struck,*
> *He hit Luciano,*
> *Quickly he hit Cortez,*
> *The witness declared.*

8th. On seeing they were injured,
They called out to God our Savior,
When sad and dejected,
They plead for justice.
9th. Anthony M. Grem
Quickly placed a complaint,
At the house of old Nel
Husband of an old woman.
10th. The special deputy was Rafaelito Garcia,
He captured the delinquent,
the night of this same day.
11th. To Chihuahua he took him,
Keeping special care,
And he placed under lock,
The drunken delinquent.
12th. On the following day,
Nicanor presented him,
Asking that they investigate him,
And the mayor provided aid.
13th. On Sotelo's part,
Gorman was the lawyer,
The judge took part,
This was well proved.
14th. The judge appointed an attorney,
On the part of the Territory,
But to speak he would not allow him,
At full view of the audience.
15th. The evidence was presented,
They saw what was declared,
The court was held and presented
through a wheeler-dealer.
16th. When the court lacked in judgment,
Everyone was amazed,
At what transpired,
A deed so worrisome.
17th. The court gave its sentence,
In a counter to justice,
There was no jurisprudence,
Everything was malice.

18th. The sentence of the court,
With malice at heart,
They gave their report,
And retired from the hall.
19th. I will speak of the injured,
Since no one partook,
Since they had friends,
They are taking them home.
20th. Their friends picked them up,
To Fernandez they are taken,
With great care,
They were assisted.
20st. When they climbed into the wagon,
Manuel Cortez and Luciano,
"Goodbye my friends," they said,
"Goodbye to my countrymen."
22nd. Cortez lowered his head,
As he traveled in the hearse,
"I am going to see the beauty,
Of my beloved homeland."
23rd. They arrived injured,
At San Fernando de Taos,
Where they were assisted,
Court was imposed.

According to the ballad, a defendant was on trial for threatening, assaulting and seriously wounding two men with gunshots fired at close range. During the course of the proceedings, once it was known that General Manuel Cortez was present, as a complainant, he was immediately apprehended and taken into custody. Manuel Cortez, ironically, was extradited by Mexico to face charges under the U.S. government for his actions in legitimate fighting of enemy forces in New Mexico during the Mexican-American War. He was returned to Taos, New Mexico, to stand trial. It is not known what became of him. But, according to the ballad, he was ready to meet his fate in his beloved homeland.

THE MEXICAN IRISH BATTALION

The most hated man in America other than Manuel Cortez was an Irishman named John Riley. He was an Irish Catholic immigrant, and Catholics were vastly discriminated against in the United States. Riley and other Irish American soldiers switched sides and fought for Mexico against the United States. The battalion numbered in the hundreds of soldiers. At the end of the war, those captured were summarily and brutally tortured and executed. This group is known as the St. Patrick Battalion, or the San Patricios, in Mexico. Many Irish Catholics immigrating to America attempting to escape famine were, upon arriving on Ellis Island, immediately recruited into the American military to fight against the "Mexican Menace." In actuality, they were enlisted to fight other Catholics in a war they knew nothing about nor understood. In the footnotes of history, it is rarely mentioned—or not mentioned at all—that some Texan soldiers bent on invading New Mexico and American troops attempting to conquer the Southwest deserted their causes and joined Mexican forces. The Irish Catholics are honored each and every year, although they are regarded as traitors to the American cause. The men are celebrated as heroes every year in Clifden, county Galway, Ireland, on September 12. In Mexico, St. Patrick's Day celebrations honor the so-called Irish Martyrs. Actor Liam Neeson and singer Linda Ronstadt have paid tribute to the San Patricios through words and song.

HUZZAH! HUZZAH! HUZZAH!!! GREAT VICTORY!

From the newspaper Sun of Anahuac, *Vera Cruz, September 1, 1847:*

32,000 Mexicans defeated by 7,000 Americans!!!
Our army has again covered itself in glory!
The English courier just arrived, and the news—NEWS we say—is, that Gen. Santa Anna and thirty thousand men have been defeated! Whipped!! And completely routed!!!
Our troops engaged those of the enemy about three miles from the capital of Mexico, where they were strongly entrenched. After a combat of TWO HOURS, they (the enemy) were put to flight!!!
The enemy's forces amounted to THIRTY-TWO THOUSAND MEN! And our forces to SEVEN THOUSAND!!!
Three more cheers for the American army: Huzzah! Huzzah! Huzzah! The enemy's thirty-two thousand men were driven to the gates of the city of Mexico by our seven thousand at the point of the bayonet.

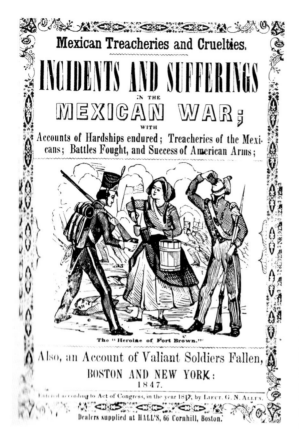

Propaganda justified a war. In this rendering included in an 1847 booklet by Lieutenant G.N. Allen published by Halls, 66 Cornhill, Boston, Mexicans are portrayed as treacherous and cruel. *Author's collection.*

One method employed throughout history to defeat the enemy has been to break down the popular perception of its leaders. This occurred during both the attempted Texan and the successful American invasions of New Mexico. Popular leaders, such as Governor Manuel Armijo and Padre Antonio José Martínez, were portrayed by propagandists as cruel tyrants who placed their own self-interests above all—at the expense of the poor people of New Mexico, who had no idea they were being used and abused by their own leaders. It was an excellent way to divide a people through words and writing and to ensure a complete conquest leading to American takeover of New Mexico's vast territory for the future interests of the United States.

PART II
CAUSE AND EFFECT

9

PAIN AND SUFFERING

It is painful enough to discover with what unconcern they speak of war and threaten it. They do not know its horrors. I have seen enough of it to make me look upon it as the sum of all evils.
—*Stonewall Jackson*

Colonel and later Brigadier General Kearny, commissioned and upgraded during his service in New Mexico after his apparent defeat and conquest of the territory, made it very clear to New Mexicans: "Resistance will be met with severe retribution."

After the conquest of New Mexico, American forces were determined to destroy anything that might be useful to the enemy. It had been a hard-fought war in New Mexico. The Missouri volunteers often went unpaid, so they attempted to supplement their meager earnings through the spoils of war. Violence was meant to convince New Mexicans they could not win the war and their Mexican government would not protect them. Americans under Colonel Sterling Price burned every town or village that did not cooperate. Undisciplined Missourian volunteers committed atrocities, and wartime sexual violence by American combatants during the Mexican-American War was common. American troops forced Mexican women into prostitution. (When Colorado volunteers arrived in New Mexico to fight Confederates during the American Civil War, the town of Loma Parda was known as an enclave for prostitution.) During the Mexican-American War, much of what took place in New Mexico was meant to humiliate the enemy. The prizes of war included the confiscation of property or seizing lands.

Rare photo showing a grandmother with granddaughter holding rosaries and a prayer book. Families suffered the loss of loved ones in the Mexican-American War. *Author's collection.*

Fort Union Trading Post established in 1828 on the Missouri River served fur trappers. Guns were traded with Plains Indians who committed depredations in New Mexico. *Author's collection.*

FORT KEARNY

In the early 1840s, Stephen Watts Kearny had established a trading post at Table Creek in Nebraska that he called Fort Kearny. This post was planned to deal with the Indians. Kearny ordered his men to escort American immigrants into various western areas and, due to his experience as a trader on the trail, was selected to lead what became known as the Army of the West into New Mexico and California. Mexicans already knew Kearny as an average soldier/merchant. His leading a force for invasion was an unexpected turn of events.

Meanwhile, everyday Americans were experiencing the loss of loved ones or their suffering due to the horrendous conflict. In addition to the battles, disease was rampant. This prompted some of them to write about heartbreak or the ravages of war, such as the following:

PEACE AND WAR

By an unlettered youth,
The Anglo American, *1847*

WAR

Town deserted; burning village;
Murder; rape; destruction; pillage;
Man compelled man's blood to shed;
Weeping; wailing; want of bread;
Commerce checked; grave citizens
Armed' with swords instead of pens;
Harvests trampled; homesteads burned;
This is war! Why is not spurned?

PEACE

Busy towns and happy village;
Fruitful fields by careful tillage;
Smiling wife, and children gay;
Labor singing through the day;
Bounteous harvests; busy farms;
Rusty swords; disused firearms;
War's vainglory set at not;
This is peace! Why is not sought?

Praying over a seriously wounded man. Innocent victims of the Mexican-American War were the old, women and children. Unknown photographer and date. *Author's collection.*

Lieutenant J.W. Abert wrote a report on January 27, 1847. In it, the American lieutenant mentions terrible ordeals the Indians were experiencing due to the scarcity of game along with their starvation:

> *Near sundown an Arapahoe chief arrived, named by whites "Long Beard." He paid me a visit, and in the evening I went to return the compliment. His lodge was the most luxurious habitation I had seen for a long time; and a few pieces of bark in the middle of the lodge kept it perfectly warm. Long Beard, Finding out that I belonged to the "soldiers," produced a gilded epaulette which had been presented to him at Bent's Fort; he also showed me a scrip of paper, signed by Mr. Wm. Bent, which paper mentioned "Long Beard" in the highest terms of commendation.*
>
> *This chief spoke a great many Spanish words, which enabled him self understood. He told us the snow was so deep that our mules could only nip the heads of the tallest grass, and begged us not to attempt to proceed, as there was no grass, and no buffaloes in the direction we were going, and that the scarcity of the necessaries of life had forced him to leave that portion of the country, where his children and his horses had been starving for some time past, and that he was now in search of meat for his people and grass*

Left: Captain Richard Weightman was an officer under Kearny. He was a delegate to the U.S. Congress and worked closely with Special Indian Agent Charles Overman. *Author's collection.*

Right: A Comanche chief. Spanish and Mexican officials pacified warring tribes. American traders sold Indians weapons, munitions and hard liquor for profit. Everyone paid. *Author's collection.*

for his animals. While we were here we saw the squaws kill a fat puppy, and having singed the hair, they put it into the pot for supper. Dogs are considered a "bon bouche," only to be served on festal occasions, but rather than starve, poor Long Beard was obliged to be this extravagant. It was well he kept his fat dogs under his eye, or some of my party might have been tempted to commit similar extravagances.

New Mexico Congressman-at-Large Richard Hanson Weightman delivered a speech in the House of Representatives on March 15, 1852, in which he reiterated the conditions in New Mexico. He stated,

Exposing the character of the Military Government, which harassed, oppressed, and plundered the people of New Mexico, and the machinations of the American and Foreign Anti-Slavery Society to stir up New Mexicans, by false representations and promises, to treason and rebellion against the government of the United States....We in New Mexico have suffered too much already, by having our soil made use of by others as a political battlefield over which to settle the slavery question, to again permit it to be so used if we can avoid it. It is, I believe, the fixed determination of the people to take no sides on this question, which in no way practically concerns them. Slave labor will not pay in New Mexico…at least one officer, of the army was in company with a number of armed men, (not soldiers,) who were engaged in acts of violence which did intimidate the people.

I want every one to understand where such outrages were committed in open day:

The inhabitants of New Mexico since February 24, 1848, have groaned under a harsh law, forced upon them in time of war, when they were thought undeserving of confidence.

The military is independent of and superior to the civil power.

The inhabitants have no voice or influence in making the laws by which they are governed.

Some power other than the Congress of the United States, has made judges dependent on its own will alone for the tenure of their offices, and the amount and payment of their salaries.

Some power other than the Congress of the United States has subjected us to a jurisdiction foreign to the Constitution and acknowledged by our laws.

We are taxed without consent, and the taxes, when collected, are not applied to the public benefit, but embezzled by officers irresponsible to the people.

No public officer in New Mexico is responsible to the people. Judges, unlearned in the law, decide upon life, liberty, and property. The full extent of the power to control and injure, which the unrestrained and organized band of office-holders-wielded, can only be understood when it is known that the military commander held to no accountability…civil officers charged with assaults upon the religion of the country, and embezzlement of the public funds.…

As it is, a de facto government obtains here of a most anomalous character, having no parallel in our history, opposed to the spirit and genius of our institutions and laws, and unrecognized by any competent authority. This government de facto was established under the laws and usages of war…and now I ask, is it extraordinary, that the Catholic clergy of New Mexico have taken a part in politics?

Imagine, if you can, Mr. Speaker, either of the political parties here to have assailed any religious denomination in the United States—the Methodists for instance—as the Catholics in New Mexico were assailed; and let me ask, if you would be surprised to see the clergy of that denomination raise their voices against the party who thus outraged their rights, and the laws of the country?

Since the arrival of the American troops in this country, a Secretary of Territory and acting Governor has suspended, Mr. Juan Felipe Ortiz, from his ecclesiastical functions as Vicario; threatened to banish a priest, who suggested a doubt as to his power to do so; and finally ordered that the priest to take advantage of the first opportunity to leave the country.

The 1848 Treaty of Guadalupe Hidalgo, which essentially ended the war still actively being fought in New Mexico and other areas of the Mexican Republic, was meant to ensure the rights and protection of Mexicans after the end of the war. This meant the protection of lands owned by the Mexican inhabitants who lived in conquered areas, their civil rights, freedom of religion and all other basic "American birthrights" guaranteed under the Bill of Rights. New Mexicans were to experience freedom of speech, the right to keep and bear arms and due process of the law. There were to be no unreasonable searches and seizures, no quartering of soldiers without the

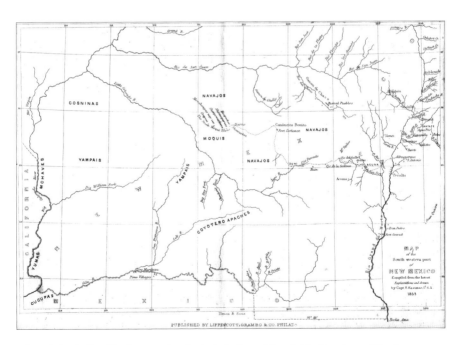

Map of the Indian Territory under the jurisdiction of Special Indian Agent Charles Overman, appointed by Governor James Calhoun. Overman was killed and scalped by Indians. *Author's collection.*

María Estefana Martínez, Padre Martínez's sister, provided assistance to all those in desperate need during the bloody fighting of the Taos Massacre by Americans. *Author's collection.*

owners' consent, no cruel and unusual punishments, no excessive fines, and guaranteed allowances for speedy and public trials.

During the outset of the Battle of Taos, wherein Taos Pueblo Indians revolted against the American presence, Narcissus Beaubien was killed and scalped. Charles Beaubien, Narcissus's father, had been appointed as a judge of the Supreme Court of New Mexico Territory by Colonel Stephen Watts Kearny. Charles Beaubien was a French Canadian who had lived in Missouri, and he was involved in the fur trading business. In 1823, he was licensed by William Clark, of Lewis and Clark fame, to trade in Indian Territory. He moved to Taos, New Mexico, where he applied to become a Mexican citizen. After his son's death, Charles Beaubien vowed to seek revenge. His biased court, with handpicked jurors, was quick to dispense judgment. What followed were rampant searches and seizures. New Mexicans were not allowed to keep and bear arms. Cruel and unusual punishment inflicted included hard labor. The American government in Santa Fe levied excessive fines. Soldiers were quartered in homes without property owners' consent. Judge Charles Beaubien ordered wholesale hangings of Taos citizens who did not understand or speak English. This prompted Padre Martínez to charge Beaubien with "endeavoring to kill all of the people of Taos" in reprisal for his son's murder. The lands of those convicted and those believed to be conspiring against the American government were confiscated. The persecution of New Mexicans continued.

10

LOSS OF LANDS

We came over Santa Fe. You could look down on La Bajada Hill.
As I looked down, I saw all these army tanks and trucks, and I thought,
what in the hell is going on here?
—Governor David Cargo, on returning from a plane trip
to Michigan on June 5, 1967

Governor Cargo discovered his lieutenant governor, Elias Lee Francis, had mobilized the New Mexico Army National Guard and had placed the New Mexico Air National Guard and its fighter planes on standby in order to deal with a national crisis developing in New Mexico. It was a question over land rights. This land struggle had a long history.

Fresh out of high school, I became a member of the Alianza, a movement inspired by civil rights activist Reyes López Tijerina. In time, this group numbered in the thousands. One of its motivations was to help New Mexicans who were living at the poverty level, who had their human rights disregarded. Another primary objective was to reclaim millions of acres of New Mexican Spanish and Mexican land grants that had been taken over by the government and wealthy, well-connected opportunists. In my own family, we had titles of ownership to the Nicolás Duran y Chávez Land Grant dating to the 1700s. My father possessed many documents that substantiated the claim, so he encouraged me to join the group. I became very involved, traveling with Tijerina and his civil rights attorney during the land grant leaders' inspiring speeches. As a teenager, I was awestruck!

Tijerina's attorney had worked as James Howard Meredith's civil rights lawyer. Meredith was an African American civil rights activist who was admitted as a student to the then segregated University of Mississippi. Robert Kennedy was one of Meredith's supporters. This all made national news. I was very active in the land grant movement, but I was also a member of the air national guard in a trained unit, ready to be activated at a moment's notice.

In history, many bloody wars have been fought even for a strip of land. After the Treaty of Guadalupe Hidalgo—which guaranteed the rights of land ownership to the vanquished Mexicans living in New Mexico and the Southwest—was signed in 1848 between the United States and Mexico, serious troubles began.

New Mexico territorial governor William A. Pile (1869–71) made quite a name for himself. When he took office, Pile ordered his close friend Territorial Librarian Ira M. Bond to destroy as many New Mexico archives as he could. A bonfire was held in the town square, and Governor Pile also used Spanish and Mexican documents to start fires in the Palace of the Governors' fireplaces. These old documents included recorded land titles to properties held by Mexican citizens in the territory for generations. Without these chains of title, everything that was recorded—and if not on record, proving ownership—was automatically in dispute. Land surveyors who had also worked closely with previous American governors and Governor Pile manipulated boundaries.

Governor Pile was an active member of the notorious Santa Fe Ring. This was a group of corrupt American New Mexico territorial officials that included judges, lawyers, bankers, merchants, traders, lawmen and politicians. The Ring held sway in New Mexico, and its power went all the way to the office of the United States presidency. The aims of the Treaty of Guadalupe Hidalgo to ensure land titles and respect for freedom of religion were not to be.

The struggle to regain loss of lands began almost immediately after the signing of the 1848 treaty between Mexico and the United States. The federal government had agencies such as the Bureau of Land Management, the United States Forest Service and the Santa Fe Land Office. Lands controlled by Hispanic New Mexicans since the settlement in 1598 as well as Indian lands protected by the Spanish, and later Mexican, governments were placed into U.S. government reserves. Kit Carson National Forest was created, and there were appropriations of whole towns and communities. As a result, the government displaced former Mexican citizens and many

This engraving by an unknown artist (date unknown) presumably shows George Armstrong Custer holding Indian scalps. It is a portrayal of American victory over Indians. *Author's collection*.

Indian tribes. Americans who leased land or acquired lands through Homestead Acts established large cattle ranches. The U.S. government initiated a series of Homestead Acts in 1862. Any American citizen who had not taken up arms against the United States could file an application for land, improve the land for five years and then file a deed for title.

Many former Confederates, including Captain Joseph Calloway Lea of Quantrill's Raiders, filed for homesteads in New Mexico. Lea County is named after him. William Quantrill's Confederate unit was known as the "Bushwhackers." They operated out of Missouri, and members included Jesse James and his brother Frank. In August 1863, the raiders attacked and massacred civilians in Lawrence, Kansas. The Confederates pillaged, raped citizens and burned the town. Quantrill's Raiders were trying to force Union loyalists out of Missouri. Later on, after the Civil War, the town of Berendo, in Lea County near Lea's land holdings, disappeared from the map. Alexander Doniphan and Sterling Price, who accompanied General Stephan Watts Kearny in his expedition of the conquest of New Mexico, distinguished themselves fighting for the Confederacy, and their monuments of glorification are proudly displayed in Missouri. Former Confederates following Lea's example saw New Mexico as the place to go.

The Middle Rio Grande Conservancy District was created in New Mexico in 1925. This agency was intended only to manage irrigation systems along the Rio Grande River. However, agency officials broadened their authority to determine ownership of lands, which were manipulated claims of ownerships, according to Reyes López Tijerina. District court judges upheld questionable land claims. One land dealing receiving national attention was the Tome Land Grant wherein it was determined that the sale of the land was illegal due to it being a land grant that could not be sold, but the purchase was deemed legal because the land "was purchased in good faith."

During the 1960s, a national land movement began in New Mexico dubbed "Tierra o Muerte" ("Land or Death"). Reyes López Tijerina spearheaded this movement. He had voraciously researched all documents pertaining to land titles in the Spanish and Mexican archives. Tijerina was also a national civil rights leader, working closely with Dr. Martin Luther King Jr. and César Chávez. The three often collaborated on civil rights issues affecting Americans who were victims of racism and abuse. For Tijerina, the struggle to which he dedicated his efforts was the repatriation of lands stolen by unscrupulous and powerful men during the territorial period of New Mexico's history. These men included Governor William Pile and members of the Santa Fe Ring, who appropriated millions of acres through land swindles. The Alianza Federal de las Mercedes (the National Alliance of Land Grants), led by Tijerina, quickly gained national and international attention and was featured in *New York Times* and *Newsweek* magazine. The land grant movement culminated in the infamous Tierra Amarilla Courthouse Raid, in which hundreds of New Mexicans were captured and detained. Many were placed under guard in corrals and stalls in northern New Mexico.

In the endless struggle to regain stolen land, shots were fired, and violence erupted at Tierra Amarilla, New Mexico. Land grant protestors undertook citizen's arrests of officials. Tijerina became the subject of a massive manhunt. The land grant leader was finally apprehended. He protested his innocence of any crime but was eventually convicted and sent to prison. The back of the civil rights movement in New Mexico was broken, but the wholesale loss of lands issue that took place during the territorial period of New Mexico history still remains unresolved, although various government commissions have been assigned to study the issue.

PADRE MARTÍNEZ, A VOICE CRYING IN THE WILDERNESS

In New Mexico, there is a famous Spanish *dicho* (a proverb or saying) that when Americans arrived in New Mexico seeking a better life, or fortune, locals accepted the foreigners with open arms and hospitality. Locals said, "Mi casa es su casa" (My home is your home). This meant that any stranger, no matter where he or she came from, would receive a warm welcome and food and drink plus heartwarming pleasantries. In time, New Mexicans said that foreigners wound up literally taking locals at their word, and not only took their homes but their lands as well. The Catholic population of New Mexico and the clergy were not only dishonored but also ridiculed in American writings of the period. Congressman Truman Smith from Connecticut maintained,

> [The lands in New Mexico are] *under the control of the clergy to an extraordinary degree. The standard of morals is exceedingly low…the country is little more than a Sodom.…I am free to say that if all the vices which can corrupt the human heart, and all the qualities which reduce man to the level of a brute, are to be "annexed" to the virtue and intelligence of the American people, I do not desire to belong to any such Union.*

Baptismal entry of Padre Antonio José Martínez, dated December 15, 1865. The famous priest fought for equal justice while performing his priestly duties. *Author's collection.*

Trader and merchant Charles Bent stated in a letter, dated January 30, 1841, to American Consul Manuel Álvarez and concerning the priest of Taos, about Padre Don Antonio José Martínez after his return from giving an address in Durango, Mexico,

> *I shall endeavor to give such as has come to my hearing. The great Literary Martinez since his return has been the all-interesting topic. He has been kept constantly employed since he got home, retelling to his greedy admirers the great respect and attention that was bestowed on him on his last trip to Durango. He says that he is considered by all who he had an opportunity of conversing with, as one of the greatest men of the age. As a literary, an ecclesiastic, a jurist and a philanthropist and more over as he has resided in one of the most remote sections of the province entirely dependent on his own resources for such an immense knowledge as he has acquired. It is astonishing to think how a man could possibly make himself so eminent in almost every branch of knowledge that can only be acquired by other men*

of ordinary capacity, in most enlightened parts of the world but as he has extraordinary abilities he has been able to make himself master of all this knowledge by staring nature in her modest guise. He is a prodigy and his great name deserves to be written in letters of gold in all high places that this gaping and ignorant multitude might fall down and worship it, that he has considered to remain amongst and instruct such a people. It is certainly a great blessing to have such a man amongst us, these people can not help but find favor in this and the other world in consequence of having such a man lead and direct them: If the days of miracles had not gone by I should expect that God would bestow some great blessing on these people through this great man. And possibly whenever the wise rulers of this land hear of the great fame of this man they will no doubt do something for these people in consideration for the great care of this more than Solomon....I had almost neglected to mention that the great Martinez has said that the Texan's have been beaten in Coahuila and California. Wonderful! how did the Texans get there, and where were they going!!! He deserves to be crowned pope for his geographical knowledge.

Bent added in a letter to Alvarez written on February 19, 1841,

Workman and myself called on Juan B. Vigil I presented the copy of the representation he made against us. I asked him after he received it that was a copy of the one he had made to the governor. He said it was. I then asked him how dared him make such false representations against us. He denied them being false. The word was hardly out of his mouth, when Workman struck him with his whip, after whipping him a while with this he dropped it and beat him with his fist until I thought he had given him enough, whereupon I rushed him off. He ran for his life....He had provided himself with a Bowie Knife for any person that dare attack him, and setting the word to the action, drew his knife to exhibit. I suppose he forgot his knife in time of need. I called on William Lee this morning respecting what he had said against us...he denied the whole, and made many acknowledgements. He is a man you can't pin up. He is a noncombatant. I presume you will have a presentation of the whole affair from the other party shortly....I doubt whether you will be able to read this. I am much agitated and am at this time called to the alcalde's I presume at the instance of Juan Vigil.

TRADING OF LAND FOR FOOD

American traders and merchants saw an opportunity to barter for much-needed commodities in exchange for land, such as what was recorded in the following. This was an easy way to increase land holdings. Unscrupulous merchants quickly became rich since not only were land holdings dealt with, but also livestock and personal possessions such as religious folk art and priceless heirlooms became part of transactions. Pueblo Indians stole from their own villages and traded items as well. Other Indian tribes dealt with American merchants for items of their own patrimony, which were listed in brochures as "Straight from Indian country." This document, from the Territory of New Mexico dated May 8, 1876, from the County of Socorro and signed by Gerónimo Armijo and Josefa Gonzales, mentions land and personal property,

> *Let everyone know by the present document that Geronimo Armijo along with his wife, Maria Josefa Gonzales, residents of Lemitar in this county and territory legally oblige themselves to mortgage their property to Michael Fischer and Arro Michaelis, merchants under the name of Fischer and Michaelis for the sum of one hundred thirty eight dollars and twenty cents. The property in Lemitar includes a house with all of its possessions, situated on the plaza, bordering on the South with the main street, on the East with adjacent property of Atanacio Abeyta, on the North with the property of Thomas Thorne, and on the West, with a public road. In addition to this house is the surrounding land. In the event that debt is not paid for whatever reason in the time allowed, along with accumulated interest, then the owners promise to transfer title and all of their rights to personal property and lands to Fischer & Michaelis.*

During the late nineteenth century, a group called the Night Riders developed. This was as a result of the barbed-wire fencing of communal lands and watering holes by Americans on the Las Vegas, New Mexico Land Grant. Prior to 1879, members of the Santa Fe Ring learned of the direction of a planned railroad system. This laying of railroad tracks would provide immense riches for the owners of the land purchased. Needless to say, finagling and the use of hired guns forced legal owners out of communities, and lands were taken.

In Spanish, the group of riders that included Hispanic ranchers and farmers was called Gorras Blancas. They wore short white cloths with two

New Mexico cowboys circa 1880. Hispanic ranchers and farmers rapidly lost lands and watering rights with the United States takeover after the Mexican-American War. *Author's collection*.

holes cut out to conceal their identities. It was a quasi-military group that counted nearly five thousand members. They issued a proclamation in an issue of the *Las Vegas Daily Optic*, a local newspaper, on March 12, 1890:

> *Our purpose is to protect the rights and interest of the people in general; especially those of the helpless classes.*
>
> *We want the Las Vegas Grant settled to the benefit of all concerned, and this we hold is the entire community within the grant.*
>
> *We want no "land grabbers" or obstructionists of any sort to interfere.*
>
> *We are not down on lawyers as a class, but the usual knavery and unfair treatment of the people must be stopped.*
>
> *Our judiciary hereafter must understand that we will sustain it only when "Justice" is its watchword.*
>
> *The practice of "double-dealing" must cease.*
>
> *There is a wide difference between New Mexico's "law" and "justice." And justice is God's law, and that we must have at all hazards.*
>
> *We are down on race issues, and will watch race agitators. We are all human brethren, under the same glorious flag.*
>
> *We favor irrigation enterprises, but will fight any scheme that tends to monopolize the supply of water courses to the detriment of residents living on lands watered by the same streams…*
>
> *Intimidation and the "indictment" plan have no further fears for us. If the old system should continue, death would be a relief to our sufferings. And for our rights our lives are the least we can pledge…*
>
> *If the fact that we are law-abiding citizens is questioned, come to our homes and see the hunger and desolation we are suffering; and "this" is the result of the deceitful and corrupt methods of "bossism."*

Two members of the Wyoming Cavalry circa 1870. Cavalrymen in New Mexico and the West were "Indian Fighters." Many Indians, including women and children, died. *Author's collection.*

Territorial Governor Edmund G. Ross, in his report of the governor of New Mexico to the secretary of the interior (contained in 1879, WPA #1036, Box 10, NMSRCA of the New Mexico State Archives) on feeling the plight of New Mexicans, wrote, "The absorption of large areas for stock ranges means the occupation of the country by dumb brutes to the exclusion of the people, where there can be no society, no schools, no roads, no improvements, no development. Under such conditions the country would be condemned to perpetual semi barbarism."

The resistance included the cutting of barbed-wire fences that were steadily being placed throughout northeastern New Mexico in areas once claimed by the Texas Republic. Barns were burned. Railroad ties made from the wholesale cutting of trees, which was creating deforestation, were also burned. Natural resources were being exploited for the railroad. Grazing lands were steadily being taken over. All of what was taking place was meant to chase the local population out of lands they had lived on for generations. Land speculation proposed to Easterners was spurred on

Woodseller in Las Vegas, New Mexico, circa 1880. After the wars, New Mexicans sold wood, made clothes, cooked or scrubbed floors to make a living. *Author's collection.*

by the Santa Fe Land Office. Brochures touting the wide availability of Indian land and former Spanish land grants were being printed to appeal to land speculators. With the passing of time, attrition broke the back of Gorras Blancas' resistance.

Padre Martínez ironically reflected on the miserable conditions of New Mexico in a letter to Mexican president Santa Anna in 1843, "Ah! There our arms have lost their honor, and our valiant fellow citizens have been degraded...who so often desired to gather laurels in New Mexico, and perhaps retake those that fell from the hands of the defenders of its streets and houses."

Through the years, several commissions were appointed by the U.S. government to study the New Mexico land grant situation stemming from the end of the Mexican-American War. To this day, the issue remains unresolved.

11

NEW MEXICANS SUCCEED

*Once social change begins, it cannot be reversed. You cannot uneducate the person
who has learned to read. You cannot humiliate the person who feels pride. You
cannot oppress the people who are not afraid anymore. We have seen the future,
and the future is ours.*
—César Chávez

AFTERMATH

With the end of the Mexican-American War, which lasted technically from
1846 to 1848, things became complicated for the vanquished territory of
New Mexico. The American conquest would take on political and religious
forms. Most New Mexicans, including Pueblo Indians, were Roman
Catholic. Suddenly, sovereignty over ecclesiastical authority was transferred
over to the United States. Officials of the Catholic Church in the United
States took advantage of this situation and transfer. They immediately
petitioned Pope Pius IX to direct control of the church in New Mexico
to the United States since Mexican and Spanish Catholic clergy had held
authority over the area for generations. Pope Pius IX, trusting his Vatican
Council, was unsympathetic toward the conquered Mexican Territory of
New Mexico and favored the United States, which was the known victor.
On July 23, 1850, Pope Pius IX proclaimed an obscure French priest
named Jean-Baptiste Lamy, with little pastoral experience, as bishop of

Frenchman Bishop Jean-Baptiste Lamy arrived in New Mexico in 1851. He spoke no Spanish or English and regarded Catholic Mexicans and Indians as unworthy. *Author's collection.*

the Apostolic Vicariate of New Mexico. Father Lamy had been struggling in a parish filled with German immigrants to the United States because of language difficulties, so he was surprised and then stunned by this unexpected elevation in his priestly career. Arriving in New Mexico along with his trusted companion Father Joseph Projectus Machebeuf, Lamy was greeted by New Mexico governor James S. Calhoun and other enthusiastic Americans. Father Lamy had met Machebeuf at the Mont Ferrand Seminary in France. They became lifelong friends. This new appointment was a challenge for both of them because they were informed beforehand that New Mexico was uncivilized.

Neither the new bishop nor Machebeuf could speak a word of Spanish. Neither could speak any other language than French, Latin and limited English. Needless to say, both of them were lost in a strange land. Lamy immediately appointed Joseph P. Machebeuf as his vicar general. Annoyingly, the two misplaced priests had to depend on the native Mexican clergy, which they were bent on replacing with French missionaries, and French nuns would later replace the Mexican nuns. Many New Mexican Catholic priests were proficient in both Spanish and English, plus some of them could speak French. These New Mexico priests were used to interacting with French traders and trappers in Taos, most of whom were Catholic. Lamy and Machebeuf were totally ignorant about the history, cultures and heritage of New Mexico, so they immediately became confrontational, searching for any excuse to boot out the Mexican priests. Some Mexican priests were accused of having mistresses. Others were charged with using the church to enrich themselves. Neither could find anything negative through their trusted spies about the famous Padre Don Antonio José Martínez.

Bishop Lamy antagonized the ancient lay Spanish Penitent orders of men and women. He freely bent church laws and used his powers of excommunication to deal with anyone and any community who opposed his wishes. This included the destruction of some Spanish colonial churches. He replaced the San Francisco de Asís Church in Santa Fe, built in the 1700s, with his French-style cathedral. He accomplished this through forceful tithing of the poor. Padre Martínez strenuously opposed these extraordinary actions through his writings and his spoken words. For this, Bishop Jean-Baptiste Lamy, immortalized as Bishop Latour in Willa Cather's *Death Comes for the Archbishop*, censured and cast off Padre Martínez, saying he was no longer regarded as a member of the Catholic Church. Anyone who sided with Padre Martínez, whether individually or as a group, would also be penalized.

Vicar General Machebeuf was accused of breaking the vow of the confessional when he pointed out the outlandish behavior and sins of Mexican women and men from various church communities during his fired-up homilies. Some of the new French priests brought into New Mexico were also charged with inappropriate sexual behavior with parishioners by the Mexican priests, and one was accused of poisoning a fellow French priest. Some belligerent French nuns working with Mexican and Indian youth and

THE MEXICAN RULERS,
migrating from Matamoras with their Treasures——
LITH & PUB. BY F. & S. PALMER, 13, ANN ST., N.Y.

T. B. Peterson Agent 98 Chesnut St. Philadelphia.

The Mexican clergy was the pun of jokes and ridicule during the Mexican-American War. Around New Mexico, priests were seen as promiscuous womanizers. *Author's collection.*

children did not escape scrutiny from New Mexicans. All of these claims from the people fell on the bishop's deaf ears. The new French prelate did not want to hear any of it. He only wanted to learn about any complaints against Mexican priests, whether or not they were substantiated. On March 3, 1868, Machebeuf was appointed Vicar Apostolic of Colorado and Utah by Pope Pius IX. On August 7, 1887, this priest who had been scorned in New Mexico was elevated to bishop. He was also promoted as a hero working among the impossible natives of New Mexico in Willa Cather's 1927 novel wherein the author uses fictional names for the "good guys" and real names for the "bad guys."

Bishop Jean-Baptiste Lamy, who became an archbishop, reflected on his tenure by saying,

> *Our Mexican population has quite a sad future. Very few of them will be able to follow modern progress. They cannot be compared to the Americans in the way of intellectual liveliness, ordinary skills, and industry; they will thus be scorned and considered an inferior race. If the bishop who will follow me has not lived among the Mexicans for a long time and if he should not show a strong interest in them, they will become disheartened. Seeing themselves on the one hand under American discipline and, on the other, imagining that the Americans prefer foreigners to them, their faith, which is still lively enough, would grow gradually weaker; and the consequences would be dreadful. The morals, manners, and customs of our unfortunate people are quite different from those of Americans. With the best possible intentions, those who would not try to understand our worshippers or would become interested in their well being, would have trouble adapting to their spirit, which is almost too primitive.*

George Wilkins Kendall, in his widely read *Narrative of the Texan Santa Fe Expedition*, had written,

> *They [New Mexicans] pertinaciously cling to the customs of their forefathers, and are becoming every year more and more impoverished...in short, they are morally, physically, and intellectually distanced in the great race of improvement which is run in almost every quarter of the earth. Give them but tortillas, frijoles, and chile colorado to supply their animal wants for the day, and seven tenths of the Mexicans are satisfied.*

Dona Bárbara Chávez
de Sánchez. Bárbara
was married to Charles
Overman. The niece of
Governor Armijo, she
survived the murders of
two husbands by Indians.
Author's collection.

In September 1849, New Mexico held a convention of delegates to recommend a plan of civil government. The territory functioned as an American military department, led by a military commandant and governor. Padre Antonio José Martínez was unanimously elected to serve as president of the convention. One recommendation was that all white inhabitants residing in New Mexico on February 2, 1848, had to "renounce and abjure allegiance to every foreign prince, potentate, state, or sovereignty whatever." These inhabitants would have to take "an oath of affirmation before the superior or circuit courts of the territory, or before the circuit or district court of the United States." One would naturally suspect that renouncement of Americans' allegiance in this place and time would have to deal with the Republic of Mexico, but it was the Republic of Texas that this referred to. Some Texans who had moved into New Mexico abhorred the idea of the annexation of the Texas Republic to the United States. The boundaries of New Mexico would be defined as "bounded north by the Indian Territory; west by California; south by the boundary line between Mexico and the United States; and east by the state of Texas."

An agreement dated Christmas Day, December 25, 1849, between Richard H. Weightman and Indian agent Charles Overman. Both agreed to represent Indian depredation claims. *Author's collection.*

In 1850, a constitutional convention was held in Santa Fe to push for New Mexico statehood. Former special Indian agent Charles Overman served as a delegate, as did Ceran St. Vrain, Richard Hanson Weightman and future governor Donaciano Vigil. Weightman was selected as one of the first senators to represent New Mexico in Congress. The Organic Act of 1850, which formally established the Territory of New Mexico, essentially tabled statehood for New Mexico. When it became the forty-eighth state in 1912, New Mexico was divided in half to also create the state of Arizona. In the Organic Act, Texas and its representatives were provided with full jurisdiction and decision making as to what Texas would accept, or not accept, when it came to the former claims of the Texas Republic over the territories of New Mexico. The U.S. government, therefore, granted several concessions to the State of Texas with the passing of the act by Congress. The concessions included:

> *The United States, in consideration of said establishment of boundaries, cession of claim to territory, and relinquishment of claims, will pay to the state of Texas the sum of ten millions of dollars in a stock bearing five percent interest....And provided, further, That, when admitted as a state, the said territory, or any portion of the same, shall be received into the Union, with or without slavery.*

News concerning New Mexico appeared in an issue of a newspaper called the *Massachusetts Spy*. Published in Cambridge, Massachusetts, this newspaper reported concerning California on March 20, 1850:

> *It was insisted that the admission of California shall be attended by a compromise of the Slavery question....California must come in whether Slavery stands or falls in the District of Columbia, New Mexico, California, or even in the Slave states....California, which, four years ago, was scarcely inhabited, quite unexplored, and almost unknown except for its capacious harbor...Today she is a State more populous than the least and richer than the greatest in the Union, for admission into which she was now applying, while Congress was debating the dissolution of that union itself.*

Mark Twain's character Mulberry Sellers states, "There's gold in them thar hills" and, rest assured, "there's millions in it." The discovery of gold at Sutter's Mill in 1848 changed the course of Indian history forever in California, parts of which had been New Mexico Territory. The 1849 California Gold Rush was a glorious boon to gold-hungry Americans seeking wealth, glory and fortune. Gold hunters called "forty-niners" swarmed into California. This precipitated the genocide of many California Indians. California governor Peter Hardeman Burnett proposed literal extermination of Indians as the only way to deal with the "Indian problem," for they populated areas miners sought to go into. "That a war of extermination will continue to be waged between races until the Indian race becomes extinct must be respected," said Burnett. Native Americans were randomly shot, killed and scalped as a result of the governor's mandates. Indian scalps sold at a premium. In her article "California's Little-Known Genocide," published by the History Channel on November 16, 2017, Erin Blakemore writes, "In 1850, around 400 Pomo people, including women and children, were slaughtered by the U.S. Cavalry and local volunteers at Clear Lake north of San Francisco." The American settlers and miners wiped out more than 80 percent of the peaceful indigenous people within two decades. Before that, hundreds of thousands of Indians populated an area they had lived in for several thousand years. The *Daily Alta California* newspaper reported, "Whites are becoming impressed with the belief that it will be absolutely necessary to exterminate

"Forty Niner's!" In 1849, American treasure seekers invaded New Mexico and California. Gold was discovered at Sutter's Mill in California. Indians sacrificed for gold! *Author's collection.*

Kit Carson. The famous trailblazer had a sinister reputation as an Indian hunter and the cruel leader of a Navajo "Trail of Tears." Many Navajo died. *Author's collection.*

the savages before they can labor much longer in the mines with security." White settlers were provided with the ability by law to enslave Indian children, and the enslavement of thousands of Indians occurred. Settlers were paid for stealing the horses belonging to the Indians they killed. Constant rapes and beatings also took place as a result.

In 1855, California enacted the Greaser Act. This law authorized local militias to terrorize and keep Mexican residents at bay. They could confiscate Mexicans' property and seize both Mexican and Indian lands by stretching and taking the law into their own hands. Later in New Mexico, the Navajo Long Walk took place. Colonel Kit Carson led a campaign to permanently subjugate the Navajo Nation. In 1863, Carson ordered the total destruction of all of the Navajo Indian food supplies, including fruit trees and livestock. His plan was to have the Indians either surrender or be shot. Those who surrendered were placed on a forced march to Bosque Redondo (Fort Sumner), where they would be imprisoned. In both the dead of winter and the blistering heat of summer, aged Indians, pregnant women and children who could not keep up due to sickness, hunger, thirst or starvation were simply shot and killed. This was a despicable page in New Mexico's history.

NEW MEXICANS IN AMERICAN DEFENSE

We, are Americans when we go to war, and when we return, we are Mexicans.
—*U.S. senator Dennis Chavez of New Mexico*

During the Civil War in New Mexico, Hispanic New Mexicans gloriously answered the call to serve and save the Union. About twelve thousand or more New Mexicans enlisted. For the most part, they provided their own arms and provisions as they fought the Texas Confederates in skirmishes

"Scalp Hunter." It is disputed whether Indians or the English began scalp taking. Both the English and American governments offered money for proof of death. Scalps were proof. *Author's collection.*

Vicenta Lavadie de Chávez, wife of Lieutenant Colonel Manuel Antonio Chávez. Carte de visite, unknown photographer, circa 1864. Vicenta feared she would be a widow. *Author's collection.*

and battles. These courageous soldiers saved the Southwest for the Union, thereby helping the United States of America to survive as a country. The Confederate government planned to have ports in California, control the goldfields of Colorado and shore up the faltering economy of the Confederacy with the takeover of New Mexico. The Confederate government wanted to annex the Southwest and the northern states of Mexico into the Confederacy. By taking over desirable ports, the Confederate navy could be launched and militarily challenge Union forces.

The regular Union soldiers left New Mexico to fight in the East. This left New Mexico Territory vulnerable to conquest by the South. The Texas Confederate troops took over Mesilla, New Mexico, and made it the capital of the Confederate Territory of Arizona. They fought an intense battle at Valverde, where many soldiers of both sides died in battle. New Mexico captain Rafael Chacón, in his memoirs, wrote that so many men died fighting on the banks of the Rio Grande River and fell to its waters that the river ran red with the blood. Those delegated with the responsibility of picking up body parts, dead bodies and the wounded for treatment and the burials of the dead are the unsung heroes of wars. For the most part, the dead were placed in quickly dug pits and piled one upon the other. Some may not have even been dead, but they died once they were rapidly buried. The graves were unmarked, and wives and families never knew what became of their loved ones or even if they could still be alive. Mourning beloved was common and ever present. The use of *memorias*, memorabilia also called memento mori, or mementos of the dead, abounded during the Civil War and well into the Victorian era.

When authors write about war and its effects, they never write about the roles of those who provided vital support to the troops. New Mexico was blessed to have Hispanic medicine women known as *curanderas*, or healers. Many of the medicinal herb and root remedies they used became ingredients now used in modern-day medicines. Medical technology in the American states was very poor and backward. In fact, unorthodox treatments such as leeching, animal dung and snake oils were commonly used. These selfless Spanish and Mexican women were dramatic forerunners to nurses. They helped and assisted wounded soldiers, both Union and Confederate. These very courageous Hispanic women did not view the Confederates as the enemy, but only as injured and hurting men who required their medical attention.

The North and the South

Major Ramón T. de Aragón, the subject of a book titled *The Chronicle of a Confederate Surgeon*, served as a regimental surgeon in the Confederate Army of Tennessee. His career began by operating a medical practice in the city of Memphis. Later on, he became the chief surgeon of General Matthew Duncan Ector's Texas and North Carolina Brigade and the Army of Tennessee. De Aragón, among many other doctors, operated under the most extreme conditions while attempting to treat the wounded and save lives during battles. Quite often, they had to amputate bloody and mangled limbs from soldiers who were severely wounded. Streptococcal infections known as hospital gangrene were common as a result of wounds. Lead, mercury and other poisonous chemicals such as calomel and quinine were used. These highly toxic chemicals sped up the deaths of the wounded. Amputations were common, so this prompted the writing of a ditty—along with a none too complimentary illustration:

> *"To The Surgeon"*
> *Ho! Ho! Old saw bones, here you come,*
> *Yes, when the rebels whack us,*
> *You are always ready with traps,*
> *To mangle, saw, and whack us.*

The word *sawbones* was popularized to reflect the constant amputations of limbs on the battlefields where everything was chaos, including the dying and the burial of the dead. The scene was unimaginable, except to those who were there and who continuously suffered from nightmares after the war. The use of anesthesia was for the most part unavailable to Americans practicing medicine. Medicine women used leaves of a plant called marijuana as an anesthetic in the Spanish Southwest. They also used other remedies that helped to prevent infection. These curanderas were accustomed to treating illnesses and wounds for generations, and they had and maintained a system of prescriptions for any and all ailments, in contrast to most English and American medical practitioners.

MUSIC AND DANCE

First Lieutenant Inocencio Martinez, who served with Company C, Third New Mexico Mounted Infantry and Adjunct of Battalion during the Civil War, was a drummer and bugler. Inocencio was born in Taos, New Mexico, on December 28, 1828. He died on May 19, 1893. His musical training began when he fashioned his own violin from a wooden box and makeshift strings gathered from a trader on the Taos plaza. His father, Santiago Martínez, felt that his son spent too much time plucking away at his instrument, so he took it and broke it. By seeing and learning from other musicians in and around Taos, Inocencio had also made his own harp out of sheep guts. Santiago's brother, Padre Don Antonio José Martínez, scolded him and ordered a real violin for his nephew from an American merchant. Sometime later, the merchant arrived in Taos from a trip to Missouri with the new violin. Inocencio was ecstatic. According to family history, Inocencio learned to read musical notes and composed his own music. He had a love for music from early childhood that grew through the years. When he attended Padre Martínez's Our Lady of Guadalupe bilingual school in Taos, he mastered English. He once asked the priest, "What form is the American government?" The wise priest responded, "Let us pretend that the American government is a burro, but in this instance it is not the clergy riding the burro, but the lawyers." Padre Martínez sponsored and promoted Inocencio's musical talents. As a young man, Inocencio Martínez became an interpreter during the first legislative session under the American government. He learned to play additional instruments, and when he enlisted for service during the Civil War, he was ready, willing and able to play reveille for the troops with his bugle and help with their marches by playing drum rolls, always inspiring the soldiers on to battle against the Confederates. Inocencio marched at the Battles of Valverde and Glorieta, not firing a shot but always being around with his musical talents spurring the troops on in battle.

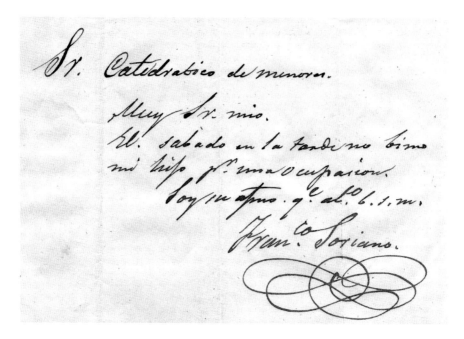

A note to teacher Padre Martínez. An undated message by Francisco Soriano advises his son couldn't attend school because he was busy. *Author's collection.*

A family anecdote recalls that he played one of his favorite waltzes on his violin, saying, "This is one of my favorites. This is the way those little musicians of mud ruined it." He referenced the way American beaver skin and fur traders arriving from Kentucky and other southern states played their fiddles in early Taos. Then he would play the violin his way. After the Civil War, Inocencio Martínez became a very popular musician and *maestro de la danza*, a dance master who conducted social dances throughout New Mexico, entertaining people with his talents and recollections of the war. At an advanced age and hoping that what the people listened to and loved would be preserved for future generations, he wrote a chronology of popular music in New Mexico. He was a progenitor of a genre now called New Mexico Hispano, or Latino, music. Some of his original compositions are still not only played today but have been incorporated into modern Hispanic popular music. The following excerpt is germane to this book in that it includes a musical transition between important periods of territorial history. Martínez's *New Mexico Musical History* has been collected for the reader with the main points out of nearly 200 notations. It is not written in chronological order by year, but only as he remembered it:

Memories of past times, derived or emanating from the age of candor and my musical notions, vestiges taken from the first day of January 1838, continuing until the first of January 1889. The following containing the first musical rudiments, ecclesiastical hymns, popular hymns, extravagant sonnets, popular melodies, long dances, round dances, wide dances, and narrow dances, Italian dances, spread out, quadrilles, and polkas, national pieces, and national anthems, marches, counter-dances, cotillions, ancient and modern, schottisches, and waltzes. Pieces for the violin, guitar, harp, flute, the piano, and organ, stork comb cylinder, of metal wind instruments, of glass, of water, with sounds of hail, fire, whistling, and foreign musical inventions from different countries. These pieces and information are exclusively written by me, Inocencio Martínez from my past life experiences from the age of twelve until the present year, 1889.

Sonnet by Padre Antonio José Martínez in 1838 on a wind cylinder.
Talión musical piece by Padre Martínez, in 1840, vernacular, sorrowful wailings.
Dance of the Eagle by Don Antonio José Ortiz, Independence of Mexico in 1821.
Jota de California, Spanish dance with its music, by Don Tomas Lucero in 1841.
Talión by Policarpio Martínez while dismounting, in 1841, The Muleteer.
Dance by Hilario Sandoval, and Mario Bebían Madrid in 1838, Los Pandos band.
Various canticles for mass, vespers, wakes for the dead, from the sisters in the Church.
The above also by Padre Martínez, Simón Salazar, Padre Trujillo, and other priests.
Alabados, Passion songs, marches of the little angels, and alabados, hymns for wakes.
Cotillones of Quirino Ocaña, in 1841, when Julian Ledoux got married. Devil's Dream, and others from 1847.
Schottisch, El Cinco de Mayo, the Fifth of May by Higinio Cruz, commemorating the defeat of the French on May 5, 1865, in Mexico.
Valses y cunas, waltzes and cradles by Juan Casados from Tome, New Mexico and from Padre Otero, 1850.
Military songs by Don Luis Baca from Limitar, New Mexico, 1861. Remembered well.

Church pieces by Lorenzo Padilla and Juan Pedrito in Las Trampas de Nuestro Padre Señor San José de la Granjera, in 1841.

Cuna by Urban Montaño, on leaving mass on Sunday, 1843.

Valse de Ventura Trujillo a waltz at the dance of the old ones (a music festival) at Ranchitos, the summer of 1840. At the plazuela of Tata Juan María Lucero, Diego Pacheco, Tata Yia, Tata Pascual, Tata Tago, Simón Salazar, Los Pandos, Manuel Andrés Trujillo, José Francisco Martínez, Juan José Quintana El Chicharito, Miguelito L. Francisquito Vigil. It was such a wonderful time of happiness and innocence. How things change!

Pieces of Ventura Trujillo and José María in El Rancho, the summer of 1849. Attending were Mariano Jaramillo, Ventura Lovato, Solís Martínez, and Los Romeros, the old ones.

Polca del Rio Nueces, in 1850, it was a clear night with a full moon on the patio.

El Desterrado Solitario, The Exiled Solitary One a song dedicated to Manuel Cortez.

El Valse Kite Carso, The Kit Carson Waltz, from or around his time.

Polka de San Juan de los Lagos, Polka of Saint John of the Lakes, band of sixteen musicians, 1850.

Redondo de Teofilo Suazo, Embudo, New Mexico, Padre Valesy said that at the summit commemorating the battle, it was well presented.

Cuna by an uncle, Tomas Lucero, in 1838. Uncle Salvador Anaya yelled out, Que Viva, May He Long Live! He and maestro Urban cheered General Armijo and his distinguished history.

El Vaquero, The Cowboy Schottisch.

Contradanza Francesa, French Counterdance by Doña Teodora Romero; Oh Muyhn Madame!

Redondo of Athlie Smith, Indianapolis, Indiana, 1859.

Pajarito de Porfina Polka, Porfina's Bird Polka, goes like Home Sweet home.

Buffalo Girls.

Old Dan Tucker.

New Mexico traditional music and folk dance reflects its history, influences and changing times. This is evident in the historical sketch that was written by Inocencio Martínez toward the end of his career. For example, he mentions "boleros Mexicanos." The bolero was a popular dance from early Spain in which dancers traditionally used castanets, but in other areas such as New Mexico, flutes and drums kept up the beat for the dancers. Other colonial dances included the *raspa* originating in Spain and the *jota*, which came from the province of Aragon, Spain. Some of the early dance forms that were prevalent in New Mexico were progenitors of the famous flamenco dances. The *chotis*, or schottische, was a type of music and dance derived from Scotland. The varsoviana, the Girl from Warsaw and *las polcas* are polkas that originated in Poland. During the period of Emperor Maximilian's monarchy under the French in Mexico during the 1860s, various waltzes spread throughout the former Spanish territories. The *redondo* was a circle dance. *Inditas* were narrative songs and dances with Native American influences. The *Cubanas* may have indicated a Cuban influx into the music. American interaction in New Mexico with trade and commerce, plus intervention, also contributed greatly to the mosaic of music and dance, and vice versa.

American merchants and traders introduced songs into New Mexico, such as "Buffalo Girls" around 1840:

> *Buffalo gals, won't you come out tonight?*
> *Come out tonight; come out tonight?*
> *Buffalo gals won't you come out tonight?*
> *And dance by the light of the moon.*

The song and music of "Old Dan Tucker" first appeared in New Mexico around 1843. "Leather Breeches" mentioned by Martínez was introduced circa 1840. There was a type of music and dance called Fisher's Hornpipe and Durang's Hornpipe. "Carry Me Back to Old Virginny" was sung in New Mexico during the Mexican-American War in 1847, along with "Oh! Susanna" in 1848; both were sung during the Civil War as well. "Arkansas Traveler" was sung in Santa Fe around 1869, but "Soldiers Joy," "Silver Legs" and other songs of the Civil War displayed the misery and suffering produced by the fighting in New Mexico and around the country. "Soldiers Joy" dated from the eighteenth century and was sung to different lyrics according to the war that was being fought. However, during the Civil War, the words referenced the dead and wounded plus the pain and suffering that could only be, according to the lyrics, remedied with drugs such as morphine and alcohol. "Silver Legs" tells about soldiers having an amputated leg. "Hail, Columbia," from 1861, was the unofficial anthem of the United States sung by Union forces and was sung in New Mexico during the Civil War as First Lieutenant Inocencio Martínez noted in his chronology.

On January 6, 1912, New Mexico became the forty-seventh state. Part of New Mexico Territory was divided to create the forty-eighth state, Arizona, on February 14, 1912. Portions of New Mexico Territory had already been separated by the government years before. Prior to statehood and after, New Mexicans distinguished themselves under American rule.

CELEBRATED NEW MEXICANS

Lieutenant Colonel Manuel Antonio Chávez, called "Savior of the Union at Battle of Glorieta." Without Chávez's heroic tactics, the Confederacy might have won the West. *Author's collection.*

Lieutenant Colonel Manuel Antonio Chavez was the Civil War hero of New Mexico when he and his forces defeated the Confederates at the Battle of Glorieta, called the "Gettysburg of the West." Miguel Antonio Otero served as a New Mexico territorial governor from 1897 to 1906 and was also a writer. Captain Maximiliano Luna distinguished himself as a "Rough Rider" during the Spanish-American War. Ezequiel Cabeza de Baca was the first lieutenant governor after statehood and the second governor. On May 30, 1917, Florencio Armijo from Las Vegas, New Mexico, enlisted as a doughboy as American soldiers were called to arms during World War I. Hispanics fighting in Germany were often ridiculed and downplayed during this time. During World War II, Armijo's son, Manuel "Lito" Armijo, fought in Germany and his wife, Eva, was a riveter in California. Relatives of her's and others worked in a parachute factory in Las Vegas, New Mexico, to help provide parachutes for American troops fighting overseas. Hispanic New Mexican women involved in the American war effort were unsung heroes. The terrible Bataan Death March, with a forced transfer of American soldiers by the Japanese on April 9, 1942, included an inordinate number of Hispanic soldiers from New Mexico. Daniel D. Fernandez gave his life while saving his comrades in Vietnam and posthumously received the Congressional Medal of Honor.

Statue of Dennis Chávez in Rotunda of the United States Capitol. "He finds himself now in…the hall of the great," Vice President Hubert Humphrey. *Author's collection.*

Prominent figures serving as role models for New Mexico youth after statehood include Fray Angelico Chaves, whose bronze statue is prominently displayed in Santa Fe. A widely acclaimed and accomplished writer, Chaves was internationally recognized along with Sabine Ulibarrí, who wrote about Tierra Amarilla and the agrarian struggles of the people dealing with changing cultural times. These two New Mexico sages are known as the progenitors who laid the framework for Latino writers in the United States. Other renowned New Mexicans after statehood included Aurora Lucero and Fabiola Cabeza de Baca, both writers whose subject was the disappearing early customs of their people, prevalent during the Mexican War period. United States senators Dennis Chavez and Joseph Montoya blazed their own trails. Chavez was an early civil rights leader during the 1930s and 1940s, before others followed the examples he set. Octaviano Ambrosio Larrazolo from New Mexico was the first Latino senator in United States history. Dr. Frank Angel was the first Hispanic president of a university, New Mexico Highlands University.

Padre Antonio José Martínez, New Mexico's folk hero, was larger than life. He was a dedicated priest whose purpose in promoting education among his people was so that they could retain their cultural identity and traditions while competing in a rapidly advancing society. This champion of the people died on July 27, 1867. The popular priest had not been a soldier with armor of metal, strong lance and tempered sword, but simply a protector of his people. His armor was his faith; and his weapons, a crucifix, a rosary, a small book of prayers and his pen. With these, he conquered hundreds of souls, and he was respected and loved by Native Americans who revered him as a great "Holy Man" with infinite power, the Hispanos he led and the Americans who appreciated his intellect. The famous priest was the supporter and the protector of all his people, and that is why in

Internationally recognized bronze sculptor Huberto Maestas created this ten-foot sculpture of Padre Martínez that dominates the Taos Plaza. Photo by Santiago Pacheco de Aragón. *Author's collection.*

the moment when they realized that they had lost him forever, they cried without consolation.

This priest of the people epitomized the strength, the perseverance, the hopes and the endurance of the Mexican/Hispano people of New Mexico, who not only survived the Mexican-American War on their soil but have continued to prosper and succeed in many ways.

BIBLIOGRAPHY

For Further Reading and Primary Sources

Abert, J.W. *Western America in 1846–1847: The Original Travel Diary of Lieutenant J. W. Abert, Who Mapped New Mexico for the United States Army*. Edited by John Galvin. San Francisco: Lawton and Alfred Kennedy, 1966.

Allen, James B. and Glen M. Leonard. *The Story of the Latter Day Saints*. Salt Lake City: Deseret Book Company, 1992.

American West, Special issue, *The Republic of Texas* 5, 3 (May 1968). Palo Alto, CA: American West Publishing Company, 1968.

Ashford, Gerald. *Spanish Texas: Yesterday and Today*. Austin, TX: Jenkins Publishing, 1971.

Bancroft, Hubert Howe. *History of Arizona and New Mexico, 1530–1888*. San Francisco: History Co., 1889. Reprint, Albuquerque, NM: Horn and Wallace, 1962.

Bartlett, John Russell. *Personal Narrative of Explorations and Incidents in Texas, New Mexico, California, Sonora, and Chihuahua*. New York: D. Appleton and Company, 1854.

Bieber, Ralph. *Marching with the Army of the West, 1846–1848*. Glendale, CA: Clark, 1936.

Binkley, William Campbell. "The Last Stage of Texan Military Operations Against Mexico, 1843." *Southwestern Historical Quarterly* 22, 3 (January 1919).

Borneman, Walter R. *Polk: The Man Who Transformed the Presidency and America*. New York: Random House, 2008.

Brooks, James. *Captives and Cousins: Slavery, Kinship, and Community in the Southwest Borderlands*. Chapel Hill: University of North Carolina Press, 2002.

Calvin, Ross. *Lieutenant Emory Reports*. Albuquerque: University of New Mexico, 1951.

Campbell, Ballard C. *Issues and Controversies in American History: American Wars*. New York: InfoBase Learning, 2012.

Chavez, Fray Angelico. *But Time and Chance: The Story of Padre Martinez of Taos, 1793–1867*. Santa Fe, NM: Sunstone Press,1981.

Christman, Margaret C.S. *1846 Portrait of the Nation*. Washington, D.C.: Smithsonian Institution Press, 1996.

Commissioner of Indian Affairs. Report Department of the Interior, Washington D.C. 1850.

Connelley, William Elsey. *War with Mexico, 1846–1847, Doniphan's Expedition and the Conquest of New Mexico and California*. Topeka, KS: Crane & Co., 1907.

David, W.W.H. *El Gringo: New Mexico and Her People*. Santa Fe, NM: n.p., 1938.

Davis, Kenneth C. *Don't Know Much About American History*. New York: HarperCollins, 2003.

De Aragón, Ray John. "El Conciliador: Resumen de la Vida del Padre Antonio Jose Martinez." *El Hispano* (July 1975).

———. "El Padre Martinez y el Obispo Lamy." *La Luz Magazine* (April 1972).

———. *Haunted Santa Fe*. Charleston, SC: The History Press, 2018.

———. *Hidden History of Spanish New Mexico*. Charleston, SC: The History Press, 2012.

———. "Mora Intrigue and Murder." *New Mexico Magazine* (August 1982).

———. *Padre Martinez and Bishop Lamy*. Las Vegas, NM: Pan American Publishing, 1976.

———. "Padre Martinez Memory Scarred." *El Hispano* (June 1978).

———. *Padre Martinez: New Perspectives from Taos*. Taos, NM: Millicent Rogers Museum, 1988.

Drumm, Stella M., ed. *Down the Santa Fe Trail and into Mexico: The Diary of Susan Shelby Magoffin*. Lincoln: University of Nebraska Press, 1962.

Duffus, R.L. *The Santa Fe Trail*. Albuquerque: University of New Mexico Press, 1958.

Edwards, Frank S. *A Campaign in New Mexico with Colonel Doniphan*. Albuquerque: University of New Mexico Press, 1996.

Elliot, Richard Smith. *The Mexican War Correspondence of Richard Smith Elliot.* Edited and annotated by Mark L. Gardner and Marc Simmons. Norman: University of Oklahoma Press, 1997.

Ellis, Richard N., ed. *New Mexico Historic Documents.* Albuquerque: University of New Mexico Press, 1958.

Emory, W.H., Lieutenant Colonel. *Notes of a Military Reconnaissance.* Washington, D.C. 30th Congress, Ex. Doc. Number 41, 1848.

Executive Document No. 17, California and New Mexico. *Message from The President of the United States, Information in answer to a resolution of the House of the 31st of December, 1849, on the subject of California and New Mexico.* Washington, D.C.: Committee on Printing, February 6, 1850.

Frazer, Robert W., ed. *New Mexico in 1850: A Military View, Colonel George Archibald McCall.* Norman: University of Oklahoma Press, 1968.

Galbraith, Den. *Turbulent Taos.* Santa Fe, NM: Press of the Territorian, 1970.

Gregg, Josiah. *Commerce of the Prairies.* Reprint. New York: Readex Microprint Corporation, 1966.

Griswold del Castillo, Richard. *The Treaty of Guadalupe Hidalgo: A Legacy of Conflict.* Norman: University of Oklahoma Press, 1990.

Habig, Marion A., O.F.M. *Spanish Texas Pilgrimage: The Old Franciscan Missions and Other Spanish Settlements of Texas 1632–1821.* Chicago: Franciscan Herald Press, n.d.

Horwitz, Tony. "Patriot Games: Nathaniel Philbrick Debunks the Myths about One of the American Revolution's Most Famous Battles." *Smithsonian Magazine* (May 2013).

House of Representatives. Reports of Explorations and Surveys, made under the Secretary of War, in 1853–4, according to the acts of Congress of March 3, 1853, May 31, 1854, and August 5, 1854. Washington, D.C.: A.O.P. Nicholson, printer, 1855.

Hughes, John T. *First Regiment of Missouri Volunteers. Doniphan's Expedition; Containing an Account of the Conquest of New Mexico.* Cincinnati, OH: U.P. James, 1847.

Johnston, A.R., Captain. *Journal of Captain A.R. Johnston, First Dragoons.* Washington, D.C. 30th Congress, Ex. Doc. No. 41, 1848.

Journal of New Mexico Convention of Delegates—September, 1849. Historical Society of New Mexico. Santa Fe: New Mexican Printing Company, 1907.

Karner, Thomas L. "Gilpin's Volunteers on the Santa Fe Trail." *Kansas Historical Quarterly* 30 (Spring 1964).

Keleher, William A. *Turmoil in New Mexico 1846–1868.* Santa Fe, NM: Rydall Press, 1952.

Kendall, George Wilkins. *Dispatches from the Mexican War*, edited by Lawrence Delbert Cress. Norman: University of Oklahoma Press, 1999.

Larson, Robert W. *New Mexico's Quest for Statehood*. Albuquerque: University of New Mexico Press, 1968.

Lecompte, Janet. *Rebellion in Rio Arriba*. Albuquerque: University of New Mexico Press, 1985.

Loomis, Noel M. *The Texan–Santa Fé Pioneers*. Norman: University of Oklahoma Press, 1958.

Lowie, Robert H. *Indians of the Plains*. Garden City, NY: Natural History Press, 1962.

Mangum, Neil C. "The Battle of Brazito: Reappraising a Lost and Forgotten Episode in the Mexican-American War." *New Mexico Historical Review* 72, 3 (July 1997).

Mansky, Jackie. *The True Story of Pocahontas*. Smithsonian.com, March 23, 2017.

Marcy, W.L. Report of the Secretary of War. Washington, D.C.: 30th Congress, 1846–47.

Martinez, Elizabeth, ed. *500 Years of Chicano History in Pictures*. Albuquerque, NM: Southwest Organizing Project (SWOP), 1991.

Meleski, Patricia F. *Echoes of the Past, New Mexico's Ghost Towns*. Albuquerque: University of New Mexico Press, 1972.

Mexican Archives of New Mexico. Microfilm publications of the New Mexico State Records Center and Archives, Roll 24, Frame 807.

Nevin, David, and editors. *The Mexican War*. Alexandria, VA: Time-Life Books, 1978.

Perrigo, Lynn I. *Hispano-Historic Leaders in New Mexico*. Santa Fe, NM: Sunstone Press, 1985.

President of the United States. Message on California and New Mexico, 31st Congress Ex. Doc. No. 17. Washington, D.C., 1850.

Read, Benjamin M. *Guerra Mexico-Americana (Mexican-American War)*. Santa Fe: Companía Impresora del Nuevo Mexicano, 1910.

Ricketts, Norma B. *The Mormon Battalion: U.S. Army of the West, 1846–1848*. Logan: Utah State University Press, 1996.

Rittenhouse, Jack D. *Disturnell's Treaty Map*. Santa Fe, NM: Stagecoach Press, 1965.

Robinson, Jacob S. *A Journal of the Santa Fe Expedition under Colonel Doniphan*. Princeton, NJ: n.p., 1932.

Schroeder, John H. *Polk's War: American Opposition and Dissent, 1846–1849*. Madison: University of Wisconsin Press, 1973.

Secretary of War. *Examination of the Reports of the Several Routes Explored.* Washington, D.C.: House of Representatives, 33rd Congress, Executive. Doc. No. 91, 1853–54.

Smith, Randy D. *Heroes of the Santa Fe Trail.* Raleigh, NC: Boson Books, 2006.

Sonit, Rebecca. "Of Illegal Immigration and Bloodshed—in 1846/ Celebrated Killings Highlight Dubious Path to Statehood." SFGATE Hearst Communications, June 25, 2006.

St. George Cooke, P., Lieutenant Colonel. Report of his march from Santa Fe, New Mexico to San Diego, Upper California. 30th Congress, Ex. Doc. No. 41, 1848.

Syers, William Edward. *Texas: The Beginning, 1519–1834.* Waco: Texian Press, 1978.

Twitchell, Ralph Emerson. *The Conquest of Santa Fe.* Santa Fe: Rio Grande Press, 1967.

———. *Dr. Josiah Gregg, Historian of the Santa Fe Trail*, Santa Fe: Santa Fe New Mexican Publishing Corporation, n.d.

———. *The Military Occupation of New Mexico, 1846–1851.* Denver, CO: Smith-Brooks, 1909.

Tyler, Daniel. "Gringo View of Governor Armijo." *New Mexico Historical Review* 45 (January 1970).

Vigil, Julian Josue. *1845 Census of Las Vegas, New Mexico.* Las Vegas, NM: privately printed, n.d.

Weber, David J., edit. and trans. *Arms, Indians, and the Mismanagement of New Mexico, Donaciano Vigil 1846.* El Paso: Texas Western Press, 1986.

———. *The Taos Trappers: The Fur Trade in the Far Southwest.* Norman: University of Oklahoma Press, 1980.

Wilson, John P. *Merchants Guns & Money.* Santa Fe: Museum of New Mexico Press, 1987.

ABOUT THE AUTHOR

Sergeant Ray John de Aragón served in the 150th Tactical Fighter Group at Kirtland Air Force Base in Albuquerque, New Mexico, in 1968. He was later transferred for training with the 560th Civil Engineering Squadron–Red Horse unit at Eglin Air Force Base in Eglin, Florida, where personnel trained were destined for Red Horse units in Southeast Asia during the Vietnam War. De Aragón became part of a military unit of elite warriors. He traveled in C-130 cargo planes with his M16, received combat training and was assigned to a rapid response and independent operations team to be sent to remote areas in high-threat environments worldwide to provide capability and support for the U.S. Air Force. De Aragón was ready to be deployed to U.S. airfields in Vietnam and Korea, and he served with the 6314th Transportation Squadron at Osan Air Base in Korea, providing materials and support for fighter planes operating in Vietnam. He was proud to wear the red beret of his unit and received the National Defense Service Medal for his military service. De Aragón is a recognized historian and scholar of New Mexico and instructor of Southwest history, legends and folklore at Luna Community College, New Mexico Highland University, and the University of New Mexico, Valencia Branch.